Thriving

Health Professionals: The Simple and Honest Guide to Growing Your Clinic

Katie Bell

Thriving Health Professionals: The Simple and Honest Guide to Growing Your Clinic

©2024 Thrive Health & Wellness Business Coaching Ltd

All rights reserved. No part of this book may be reproduced, stored in a retrieval system or transmitted in any form or by any means (electronic, mechanical, photocopy, recording, scanning or other) except for brief quotations in critical reviews or articles, without the prior written permission of the publisher.

ISBN: 9781068543401 Paperback

Published by: Inspired By Publishing

The strategies outlined in this book are provided primarily for educational purposes. Every effort has been made to trace the copyright holders and obtain their permission for the use of copyright material.

The information and resources provided in this book are based on the author's personal experiences. As such, any outcomes or results described are specific to the author and may not be indicative of your own experience. There is no guarantee that you will achieve similar results after reading this book.

This book is not intended to replace professional medical care or advice. Always seek the advice of a doctor or qualified mental health professional if you have any concerns about your mental or physical health.

The author reserves the right to make changes to the content and assumes no responsibility or liability for any actions taken by purchasers or readers of this material.

Dedication

For Nanna & Gromps.

Acknowledgements

Writing the acknowledgements has been the hardest part of writing this book. I really think that from the day I was born, people have taught me things every step of the way.

But starting with Dr. Hill, who was a legend of a GP back in the day and who brought me into the world, felt a bit much to start with!

To the various people who have inspired me and given me great advice at different times, the authors of the books I have read, the patients who have offered me their time, and advice, and knowledge, my business coaches who put me on this path and have been a constant source of support: Thank you.

To my team in my clinic who have allowed me the space to write this book while starting and growing a hugely successful business: Thank you.

To my team in Thrive, who challenge me, support me, have become some of my greatest friends, and encourage me to always play bigger, your input is always appreciated. Thank you.

To my writing mentor, Angela, and all the team at Inspired By Publishing, it has been a joy from day one and not a hard, painful process, which everyone said a book would be! Thank you.

To my friends, I continue to appreciate you more than you would ever know and thank you for always supporting me, pushing me, and being a constant source of fun in my life. Thank you.

Thanks to my brother, Tom, who inspires me daily and shares the "Bell" work ethic. He is always interested, he always listens, he keeps everything light and fun, and even if you stabbed a dart in my bum aged 12, we have always been incredibly close. Thank you.

To Nanna and Gromps, who allowed me to sell the entire contents of their house back to them regularly so I could play "shop."

For Gromps, who always offered a sense of risk, and for Nanna, who was the first lady to drive in Stockport (the place I was born!). For always inspiring me to work for myself, take risks, and keep my money in a tin box under my bed! Thank you.

To my mum and dad who give their everything to me and my brother. Your constant, unrelenting support and encouragement have allowed me and Tom to do what we have done and will do in the years to come.

This book is a result of you both, the lessons you have taught me, the advice you have always given, and the kindness and love you have always shown. Thank you.

To my dog, Toby, for making every day brighter, messier, and full of love. Thank you.

To my husband, Matt, who always tells me I can do it, who listens, is incredibly patient when I stack the dishwasher like I am on drugs, and supports me 110%,

110% of the time! I am excited for our future, let's see what adventures we have to come. Thank you.

Contents

Introduction	1
1 - Planting the Seeds for Success	9
2 - Unearthing Your Money Mindset	19
3 - Cultivating Confidence and Authenticity	31
4 - Pruning the Overgrowth	47
5 - Strengthening the Trunk	55
6 - Bringing the Money Branch to Life	67
7 - Branching Out	81
8 - The Growth Rings of Success	99
9 - The Leadership Canopy	109
10 - Cultivating the Systems Branch	123
Conclusion - Harvesting the Fruits of Your Clinic Success Tree	133
What's Next for You	141
Recommended Readings	144
References	145

Introduction

It was in February 2015, four days before my wedding day, that I realised I was an addict. My physiotherapy and wellness clinic had opened in November 2014, and I had not taken a breath since. I was juggling every single thing: being a physio, teaching Pilates classes, cleaning, answering the phone and emails, bookings and invoicing, plus my wedding planning on top of all that. But I was addicted. I was also, on reflection, close to burnout! That showed up a few months later. Don't worry, I didn't escape that one.

But I loved it! I loved that I was making a difference in my clients' lives, I loved answering to myself in creating a business that truly served my clients and I loved that I was finally getting the hang of the whole "running a business thing" (or so I thought!). But I was addicted – I was addicted to work. I felt like I could not drop any balls or stop spinning any plates, even for a second.

How long would I be able to sustain the hours I was putting in at that point?

After a few hard months and a wedding, I began feeling like I had a regular job again! There was none of the freedom nor flexibility I had thought running a business would give me. Something was going to have to change, and sharpish. I was then reminded of this quote by someone I have huge respect for: "Doing the same things over and over again is the definition of insanity,[1]" once said writer Rita Mae Brown. It was at that moment I committed to learning how to run my business and get myself out of being employed by myself!

Beyond being a great physiotherapist who definitely knows her stuff, I also knew what I didn't. Where do I even start there? There's how to market my business, how to manage cash flow, how to hire, how to lead; the list goes on and on. Then there was also everything I didn't know about growing and scaling a physio and wellness clinic. I wanted to create an even bigger impact on my community in Sheffield, whilst getting my life back and earning a really good living. It seemed almost impossible to have it all, but as I was addicted to work – and hard work at that – I threw myself into more hours of learning.

But what started all this? Rewind to earlier in 2014, way before I opened up shop. I was sitting at the Holiday Inn in Sheffield surrounded by that god-awful patterned carpet and a musty hotel smell. Hold the glamour! I had just been introduced to a business coach and attended their workshop on how to get more clients – not for me, but for the business I was with at the time. I remember thinking, "Why am I working for someone else? I feel unfulfilled in my work and seem to have hit the ceiling of potential income at only 28 years old, but with no flexibility and minimum holiday allowance." It was like something smacked me in the face after that workshop and woke me up! I went home and announced to my husband, "I am going to leave my job and open up my own clinic."

Now back to 2015. In my quest to take my business to the next level, I embarked on a mission to overcome the steep learning curve. I read lots of personal growth books, paid for programs and coaching, and went through a bucketload of hard work (let's keep this book real!). The word "mindset" was introduced to me, and working on this alongside my business growth activities became my focus. I came to a huge realisation that the best strategy in the world will not outperform a lacking mindset. As I changed my beliefs, my mindset shifted, and I began dreaming bigger, taking bold actions, and creating big results.

I leveraged all aspects of the clinic and within three years, we hit seven-figure sales. By 2018, I had a big team, I was working fewer clinic hours than I had ever done and we were about to double the size of our premises.

Let me roll forward to a skiing trip to Whistler in March of 2019 with my original business coach. After a day on the slopes, we hit the outdoor hot tub in minus 17-degree weather and the conversation moved to business and what was next for me. When I asked myself specifically how I had been able to grow my business to multiple six figures in the first year, achieve growth by making more profit year on year and remove myself more and more from clinic duty, I realised that I had a method.

My mission has always been about transforming lives, but I felt I was still playing too small. I knew I had more to give. I am a big advocate of our industry. We have so many incredible clinicians, but the huge lack in our training means we have fabulous clinicians and terrible business owners (2014 me included!). I knew I could impact the health and wellness of more people, and that's where Thrive was born. In the hot tub!

Why couldn't I support practitioners in the health and wellness industry to create brilliant businesses that serve them rather than starve them? Especially since with these brilliant businesses we build, we all would be positively impacting the lives of so many people? I decided I could, so I did, and here we are!

This process has now worked for hundreds of clinic owners at the time of writing this book. They have seen results like doubling to quadrupling their revenue, halving their clinic work, getting more hours to spend with their family, and doing the things they love to do. Plus, they're even able to pay themselves more than they ever believed "running a clinic" would enable them.

This is the method I have included in this book, the one that my team of coaches and I teach within Thrive and our coaching programs. But this is not about me, my team, past members, or our program. This is about you. Welcome to a journey that has the potential to transform not only your clinic but also your life. This book is about more than just running a successful business - it's about creating a thriving, sustainable clinic that brings you joy, fulfilment, and the freedom to live the life you've always dreamed of. As a clinic owner, you know that success doesn't happen by chance. It requires careful planning, consistent effort, and a deep understanding of the many facets of your business. But where do you start? How do you ensure that your clinic not only survives but truly thrives in an increasingly competitive landscape?

Enter the Clinic Success Tree, a framework designed to guide you through the process of building a strong, healthy clinic from the ground up. This method, which has been at the core of my own journey and the success of many other clinic owners, is built on a simple yet powerful idea: Every successful clinic is like a tree, with roots, a trunk, branches, and fruits that represent different aspects of your business.

The Roots of this tree are your personal performance and mindset. These foundational elements anchor everything else, providing the stability and strength you need to weather the challenges of running a clinic.

The Trunk represents your clinic's core: your values, master plan and strategy. This is where you define what your clinic stands for, where it's headed and how it will get there. A strong trunk supports the entire structure, ensuring that your clinic grows in the right direction and remains true to its purpose.

The Branches symbolise the various operational aspects of your clinic: your team, marketing, sales, operations, and numbers. These are the areas that need careful attention and nurturing to ensure your clinic runs smoothly and efficiently.

Finally, The Fruits of your Clinic Success Tree are the rewards you reap: time, energy, money, and confidence. These are the tangible and intangible benefits that come from successfully managing your clinic and achieving your personal and professional goals.

In this book, we'll explore each of these elements in detail, offering practical advice, real-life examples, and actionable strategies to help you cultivate a clinic that not only meets your expectations but exceeds them. Let's be clear: Success is not one-size-fits-all. The fruits of your labour – whether financial freedom, more time with family, or personal fulfilment – are unique to you. Throughout this book, I'll encourage you to stretch your ambitions, to dream bigger, and to create a clinic that supports the life you truly want to live. Running a clinic doesn't have to mean living an average life. It doesn't have to be about long hours, endless stress, or just getting by. With the right mindset, strategy, and systems in place, you can build a thriving clinic that gives you the freedom to live life on your own terms.

This book is your guide to planting, nurturing, and harvesting your own Clinic Success Tree. Whether you're just starting out or you've been in business for years, the principles and strategies you'll find here are designed to help you grow a clinic that's both successful and sustainable. I would also love it if you have a notebook or a journal beside you as you go through this book. I will be giving you guide questions and reflection pointers that you need to do in order to get your Clinic Success Tree flourishing. At the end, you will find links to the resources you need, as well as an invite to come chat with me and my Thrive team.

Are you ready to plant the seeds for your success?

Thank you for choosing me and trusting me on this journey. We're here if you need us to help you every step of the way.

Love,

Katie Bell

1
Planting the Seeds for Success

I know you're here because you are a clinic owner who thought running a clinic would give you more time and more money so you could focus more on family and the fun things in life. However, it's more likely you are working endless hours, feeling buried under client and admin work, stressed by the fact that some months you have too many clients and other months you don't have enough. You can never truly switch off and have what I call an unplugged holiday, and when you do take time off, the business suffers as you are a big income generator - or maybe the only one!

It might also be that you now have a team, and they've become the biggest challenge and cost in your business.

Are you wondering whether you should just run a one-man band again in your garage?

To top it all off, when you calculate what you are paid per hour you work in, and on the business, you'll likely find out you are the worst-paid person. The national minimum wage at the time of writing is £11.42, and having conducted some research at a masterclass, the average clinic owner is being paid £4.53 per hour. Oh, and you never get to take the minimum holiday of 5.6 weeks per year.

Welcome to owning and running a clinic!

I started with that because it's important, you know, I really do understand. I speak to hundreds of clinic owners every month, and I was this very person 10 years ago. I paint a sad picture here, but I also get the joy of painting a much better picture with the clinic owners I work with every day. Things do not have to be this way. That is my promise.

Before we get into the nitty-gritty of all the big fancy things you think your business needs – like a marketing strategy, a sales strategy (yes, even us in the "clinical" world need one of those), and your growth plan (you absolutely need this!) – we are going to start with the most neglected and forgotten part.

Let us start by imagining your clinic as a tree. Alan Titchmarsh, eat your heart out! Don't worry, I am not going to teach you what you should be doing in your garden. Right now, my guess is you are scrambling to fix the broken branches in your business every single day.

Staff issues, marketing mishaps, financial worries, a lack of systems and processes – the list of things to fix never ends. This will feel like you are constantly spinning a lot of plates, but nothing becomes hugely successful or gives you any time back. Nevertheless, the typical thinking is that you are a worker bee who needs to keep on spinning and working.

But what if I told you that the key to a thriving, fruitful clinic lies beneath the surface, the part of the tree we don't see, but without it, the tree dies?

The roots. It's the very foundation of your clinic, and it starts with you. And this is the *one* thing everyone forgets or thinks will change so long as they work harder. Guess what? It won't! And in case you want to test it, don't bother, I've done that for you.

I remember when I was a little girl, and my mum and dad took me to a circus, the type that would not be allowed today. The lady who sold us tickets went on to be the acrobat, the trapeze artist, the lion tamer, sold ice creams in the interval, and I can bet my mint choc chip ice cream that she was also the one who cooked and cleaned the motor homes, schooled the kids and fed the animals after the show.

When I started my clinic, I was exactly like this lady - minus the lion!

I kept working harder and harder, expecting that someday it would result in more money and more time. It didn't. It resulted in completely the opposite!

I often speak to clinic owners who honestly look exhausted. They are burnt out, drained, and frustrated, but they cannot stop. They say they have to make it work or that they are making "okay money." It feels like this is what they are all settling for this: "okay, money." But where did this come from, this idea that making an "okay" living is all we are deserving of?

The one thing I did have, which many clinic owners I speak to don't, was a coach. I also had a ridiculous work ethic, something I initially thought would separate me from the pack and make me successful.

Before I opened my one-person, two-treatment-rooms-and-a-studio clinic with no money and no clients, I made the bold decision to learn from someone who had been there and done it, who had walked the path to more time and money before me. I had no idea how I would pay for it, but I thought I had two options. First, I could try and figure this out for myself, which would take me years and a lot of money. I did not have one minute of business coaching on my physiotherapy degree, by the way, so I definitely knew that whilst I was a blooming brilliant physio, I was going to be a pretty average business owner. Right enough, it did turn out I knew next to nothing about running a successful clinic. Second, I could invest in myself. No, not with another clinical course on the shoulder, but I could learn what I actually needed to learn to run a successful business.

Remember, I had the work ethic of a bee, an ant, and a beaver in one! My initial choice was obvious.

For the first two years, business absolutely flew. I was fully booked within two weeks of opening; we made six figures in year one, I recruited fast, we added services, we grew and grew, but...

... I was tired! Exhausted! Burnt out! Battery empty! Sound familiar?

I am going to repeat what my coach said to me because I want to pay this forward and say it to you, too:

"Katie, there are two ways you can work in business: using force or using power. You have used all the force up. You literally cannot work any harder or any more hours. So, if you want different outcomes, you are going to have to start doing things differently."

Do you ever feel like you're doing the same things over and over, but the end result never changes?

And that is when I realised, I could no longer keep working on the branches. Yes, it had gotten me to six figures. Yes, it got my clinic off the ground. *But* this strategy was *not* going to give me more time and freedom. And this was the moment I was introduced to the word mindset!

Now, I chose to start here because if you look at the latest statistics on reading books, 40% of you may not make it past the first chapter. This is not because the book is not worth the read (it really is!). It's because we get distracted, we need to see another client, or we leave it on the pile of books we must read, or maybe on top of the pile of your industry magazine that lands every month and is also never read.

So, I decided I need to teach you about the one thing you really need to know. Even if you did *nothing* else, just changing this would change your life.

Getting clear on how you are wired, what your beliefs and your thoughts are, is the foundation of success. Your mindset is what is really running the show right now.

"Mindset" to me was a word being chucked about ten years ago that I honestly took with a pinch of salt. I used to think, just get on with it and graft! But then I looked at the big players – Oprah, Branson, Musk – and I remember thinking, "I am pretty sure they are not the only performers at the circus. Yes, they definitely will have earned the stripes, but to generate more freedom and money, there must be something they do differently." And this blooming mindset word came up again!

Let me introduce you to the Be-Do-Have principle. This explains how, if we move our focus from what we have (or don't have) to who we want to be and align our goals and actions with that state of being, in time, we'll achieve our "haves." "When I have, I'll do, and then I'll be," becomes, "Who must I be, and what must I do to have what I want."

I needed to focus on who I must be, and therefore, what I must do from this new place of being. Who are you being right now? Are you behaving like someone who is running a multiple six-figure clinic with freedom of time?

Feel free at this point to skip to the branches (marketing, sales, operations, team and numbers) later in the book, but please know this. Working purely on the branches will work for a little while and then eventually give you more of what you have now: no time, not enough money, and feeling constantly tied to your business.

Why We Are Our Biggest Barrier

It's a tough pill to swallow, but we are our biggest barrier to success. It's not the economy, the competition, or even your staff – it's you. Your beliefs, your habits, your fears can either propel you forward or hold you back.

Think about it. How often do you second-guess yourself? How many times have you delayed making a decision because you were afraid of the outcome? How frequently do you find yourself stuck in the same old patterns, expecting different results?

Your clinic is exactly where it is today because of your beliefs and therefore your actions. If these were not in the way, you would have already achieved what you set out to achieve.

A great way to understand where you are now, and perhaps why, is to reflect and accept. You need to take some time and think about your current situation, whether by journaling or simply reflecting. Ask yourself the questions below.

Are you overwhelmed with long hours and fluctuating patient loads?

Do you feel financially stressed despite how hard you work?

Is your focus solely on fixing surface issues like staff and marketing?

Have you considered that your mindset might be the root cause of your problems?

Do you have a coach or mentor to guide you?

Are you using force instead of strategic power to drive your clinic?

Have you explored the Be-Do-Have principle in your approach?

Are your internal beliefs and habits holding you back?

How is your mindset affecting your clinic's growth?

Are you ready to address the roots for lasting success?

So now that I have dropped this bombshell and you've had time to reflect, let's go further underground and look at your money mindset. Your money mindset has a direct impact on your income. The way you think about and handle money really shapes how much you bring in and how much you can grow.

So, before we just do more marketing and fix that branch, we really do need to start here.

2
Unearthing Your Money Mindset

Your money mindset is like the thermostat in your house – it sets the temperature for your financial life. Just as a thermostat determines how warm or cool your environment feels, your money mindset shapes your beliefs and attitudes about wealth and abundance. This mindset can range from scarcity, where money feels elusive and fleeting, to abundance, where opportunities and resources seem plentiful. Like adjusting a thermostat to change the climate in your home, shifting your money mindset is essential if you want to increase your financial well-being.

By recognising and transforming your internal settings, you can open yourself up to greater financial growth and success.

My dad had taken over my Gromp's plumbing and building business and so was self-employed. This meant that growing up, I would watch him work five days a week and every Saturday morning "on the tools," as we used to say in our house.

It didn't end there. Every evening after a 10-hour day, he would be in his office answering calls, faxes, and customer questions, and my mum would be there too, typing at the speed of light as dad dictated his customer quotation letters (after she had also worked a full day!).

They say that you should never buy anything you can't afford, and that money definitely does not grow on trees. These two sayings formed my money mindset and beliefs around hard work from a very young age. In fact, when I was little, I used to set up shop at Nanna and Gromps' place (bless my grandparents' patience!) and sell the entire contents of their own house back to them on at least a monthly basis.

Why do I tell you all of this?

Your money mindset is something you were given. Good or bad, it is shaped and based on experiences and conversations you had growing up.

The most influential years are from zero to seven years old, as is typically noted.

Everyone has their own unique experience with how the world works growing up, so all of us, you, me, everyone, go through life anchored to a set of views about how money works too. It also goes a lot deeper than this for the woo people, but that's another book and another day!

For you as clinic owners, understanding and reshaping your money mindset is crucial. This is one of the deepest roots we have to look at when it comes to making more money, but is also often the one thing buried in our subconscious and never looked at when it comes to growing a successful business.

Your money mindset directly impacts how you price your services, how much money you attract *and* hold onto and ultimately, the success of your clinic.

Having spent literally months of time on calls to clinic owners across the UK and Ireland, these are thoughts I hear on practically every call:

"Clients can't afford to pay more."

"They will all just go to a competitor if I put my prices up."

"I only change my pricing every now and again."

"I offer discounted appointments."

"My pricing is based on how things have always been done in the industry."

"I put my price up by £2."

"I'm annoyed that my hairdresser charges more than me."

"I don't make enough profit."

How familiar do these sentences sound?

Whether you think these words or say them out loud, we seem to have an ingrained perspective in the industry that physiotherapy, osteopathy, or sports therapy are low-cost services, that perhaps it should be free, or that it does not hold really high value to people and therefore we cannot possibly charge a high rate for our services. This is a complete contrast to other professions like veterinarians, consultants, and even hairdressers that have long established the expectation of paying for expertise and quality service.

I am going to say this a lot until it finally sinks in: You transform people's lives!

You offer an invaluable service to your community, you have spent literally *years* training, practising, doing more and more Continuing Professional Development (CPD) courses to stay up to date and offer a top-level service, putting the hours in and so much more. This *has* to be reflected in your charges.

So, the good news is, if you, like most people, have a troubled or conflicted relationship with money, you have the ability to transform it and become great pals with it. One day you'll wake up and you'll be living the life you've always wanted.

We have been raised to believe that you have to work hard to make money, and certainly, there are times when this is true. But the real secret is taking huge, uncomfy risks. You have to do stuff you have never done before!

I would love you to take your journal and note down anything that can come up for you around money.

We need to bring this stuff up to above the surface. Only do this if you're really serious about making more money!

Just write down anything that floats around in your head, e.g., I don't have enough money, I always save for a rainy day, I think no one has any money in this economic crisis, I don't believe we could charge any more.

Looking back at your reflections, thoughts, and beliefs are really interesting, aren't they? That's because that right there is shaping your reality right now.

The car you drive, the hours you work, the price you charge, the profit you make, the house you live in, the shoes you wear, the food you eat – all that is a direct reflection of your beliefs and thoughts. Your external world is a mirror of your internal world.

One of the biggest obstacles to making lots of money is not a lack of good ideas or time, nor is it because you are not good enough at running a business. It's that we refuse to give ourselves permission to make lots of money and become rich.

I speak to many clinic owners every week, and the standard they set themselves for personal income never fails to make me feel sad, hence the need for me to write this book and do what I do.

Why have we been conditioned to think that owning a clinic means you can't be rich?

I hear you. You want to spend time with those you love, give your time to people who need it most, spend time lying on the grass staring up at the sky and not writing patients' notes at 9pm – all things that money can't buy.

Here is my problem: When did it become an either/or situation? If you become rich, it's not like you will never be at another family party, or never be able to give an hour of your time to a kids' camp. If you do it correctly, you can do *more* of this stuff, and do it in style.

Rich, in my eyes, is about being able to afford all of the things and experiences required to fully live your most authentic life. While the amount of money you need will depend on who you are and what you desire, we exist in a world where nearly everything costs money. A healthy desire for wealth is not greed; it's a desire for life. We are all in this industry because we want to help people. We are caring, helpful people; this lights us up. But you cannot give what you have not got.

Your business must be profitable for you to live the fullest version of your life and for you to help others on a much bigger scale. Our world needs as many compassionate, creative, big-hearted people to be as rich as possible.

So, it really is important to be aware of any negative beliefs you are harbouring around money. You are meant to thrive, and by thriving you automatically help others to thrive too.

Here are the most common money mindset barriers that we see:

Scarcity mentality. Believing there's never enough money, leading to underpricing services.

Fear of rejection. Worrying that higher prices will push away clients, which often stems from undervaluing your own expertise.

Comparison trap. Comparing your prices to NHS services or low-cost competitors, instead of aligning with the value and quality you provide.

"So, Katie, I am starting to see why my beliefs are shaping my reality, but how the heck do I change them?" you might be asking. Well, there is a lot more to this that I can possibly provide in one chapter, but for a start, check out my tips below.

Value your expertise. Recognise that your skills and knowledge are worth a premium price. Your years of training, experience, and the results you provide are valuable.

Adopt an abundance mentality. Believe that there are plenty of clients willing to pay for quality care. An abundance mindset attracts opportunities and higher-paying clients. Just Google how many people live in your town, and then think about how many of them are suffering from pain. Trust me, there are enough.

Focus on value, not time. Shift from charging based on time spent to the value provided. Consider creating packages or programs that reflect the comprehensive care you deliver, rather than single sessions.

Educate your clients. Clearly communicate the benefits and outcomes of your services. When clients understand the value and impact of your care, they are more willing to invest in their health.

Invest in yourself. Just as you ask your clients to invest in their health, invest in your own growth and development. This is a key belief for me.

If I am not prepared to be coached, how can I expect people to want to be coached? It makes complete sense. If you are sitting here reading this book and you yourself are at the bottom of the priority list, you spend nothing on yourself or you don't value yourself enough to invest in, then here lies the problem in attracting clients, money, and time.

The Quantum Shift

Let me just talk about quantum physics for one second.

In the realm of vibrational energy, the principle of attraction is paramount: What you emit is what you draw into your life. It's called the Law of Attraction.

If you neglect to invest in yourself – be it through personal growth, self-care, or professional development – you inadvertently signal to the universe and those around you that you are not worthy of investment. This lack of self-prioritisation diminishes your vibrational frequency, repelling the very opportunities and support you seek.

Therefore, to attract others' investment – whether financial, emotional or professional – you must first embody that commitment within yourself. By valuing and prioritising your own well-being and growth, you elevate your vibrational energy, thereby attracting the external validation and resources you desire. I dare you to try it and see what happens!

Okay, back to earth. Here are the four steps I encourage you to do next:

1. Review your pricing. Take a hard look at your current pricing structure. Are you undervaluing your services? What would it look like to charge what you're truly worth? And remember if you raise your prices by 25% and 25% of your clients leave, you make the same money using less time.

2. Identify limiting beliefs. Write down any negative beliefs you have about money and pricing. Challenge these beliefs and replace them with positive affirmations. You get to decide what you believe, so choose something different.

3. Set financial goals. Establish clear financial goals for your clinic. Know your numbers: How much do you need to earn to cover expenses, reinvest in your business, and pay yourself a fair salary? Make that last one your first goal. Don't worry, we are going to cover your numbers later in the book.

4. Communicate value. Practise articulating the value of your services to clients. Develop clear messaging that highlights the benefits and outcomes they can expect. Stop playing it down!

By addressing and shifting your money mindset, you'll create a strong financial foundation for your clinic. This change is crucial before diving into marketing strategies and other business tactics.

Now that we've unearthed some of the mindset that has been holding us back, let's now look at the success mindset and why this is so important and often pushed down below the surface into our subconscious, too.

3

Cultivating Confidence and Authenticity

In your journey to building a successful clinic, one of the most insidious challenges you may encounter is imposter syndrome. It's that nagging voice in your head that whispers or sometimes shouts, "You're not good enough." What I have come to realise is that it's a common phenomenon among high achievers. If you are reading this book, then it is highly likely you are one.

I am a physiotherapist "by trade" as I like to call it, a recovering people pleaser and also a recovering work addict, as you now know! I missed an A in Biology A-level by two points, meaning I did not get my points to get into university. This meant resitting the year whilst working for British Airways (which is a whole other story!) and eventually heading to university one year later.

There were 100 applicants for every place when I eventually started applying. For as long as I can remember, I have always been a hard worker, always achieving in sports and school. And while I was not liked by everyone – as high achievers often aren't – I did wish I was, so this knockback really affected me. I almost did not pursue the career I had always wanted to. But you know how the rest of the story goes. I get the pleasure of speaking and coaching hundreds of clinic owners in a variety of ways, and imposter syndrome is never far away in any situation they find themselves in.

My hope from this chapter is that you become more aware of your own imposter syndrome. I promise you it's there, somewhere below the ground. If it wasn't, you would all be living your Level 10 life!

For reference, a Level 10 Life is achieved when you can give the different aspects of your life – including your environment, hobbies, health, relationships, and finance – a perfect rating. That is, a 10 out of 10! So, let's give it the space in this book, delve into what it is, how it manifests, and most importantly, how you can overcome it to foster a thriving clinic and a confident mindset.

What the Heck Is Imposter Syndrome?

Imposter syndrome is a psychological pattern where we as individuals doubt our accomplishments and can translate into a persistent fear of being exposed as a fraud. This is despite the fact that we have loads of evidence to show we are not only competent but blooming amazing at what we do! It crops up knowingly, and often unknowingly.

Those of you experiencing this syndrome remain convinced that they do not deserve the success they have achieved. This mindset can be particularly detrimental in the context of running a clinic, where confidence and authenticity are crucial for building trust with clients and staff, but imposter syndrome can manifest in so many weird and wonderful ways.

One of our amazing clients in Thrive is doing all the work. She is following everything we are encouraging her to do, and her business has grown. She has more team members, more revenue, more profit, she is paying herself more and she has more time to work on the business. "Great, Katie. What is your point?" you ask. Well, things on paper look great, but she recently has had people leave the business, she is back covering reception for some hours, she has a tricky staff member and the cleaner has started doing some random stuff.

This is what we in the industry call self-sabotage. It's a sneaky chuffer because it's often a subconscious behavioural pattern where an individual hinders their own success and well-being. This means we don't often know we are doing it until someone like Philippa, our mindset and success coach, spots it!

Self-sabotaging behaviour can come from imposter syndrome or fear of success. So, we may have the best master plan and marketing tactics for our business, but achieving consistency and success in business means dealing with this powerful stuff first!

This client is now aware of her unconscious pattern. She is repelling success and more money away because of some deep-rooted beliefs. But we're working with her on it.

Let's take a pause... Take a moment to grab your journal. I find when I am reading that things can come up for me, and it's important to not push them back down.

Think about what may have popped up from your own life while reading this chapter and write them down. Here are some questions to prompt your thoughts:

Where are you not living the best version of my life? Think about different factors like health, relationships, business, money, confidence, rest, spirituality, and whatever else you'd like to highlight.

What happens when you hit success or an achievement? Do you just brush past it, or do you start doing stuff to sabotage it?

Do you classify yourself as a high achiever? Don't be modest here!

The Different Faces of Imposter Syndrome

Imposter syndrome can show up in various ways, often disguised as different aspects of self-doubt and insecurity. Here are some of the common manifestations we see in clinic owners.

Perfectionism

You set impossibly high standards for yourself and feel like a failure when you can't meet them. This can lead to overworking, burnout, and constant dissatisfaction with your performance. You procrastinate endlessly because things are not quite perfect, meaning you don't get an awful lot over the line, boxed off, done, and dusted!

Overachievement

You may feel the need to work harder than everyone else to prove your worth. While this can lead to success, it often comes at the cost of your well-being and can create an unhealthy work-life balance. This is something I see and hear a lot: clinic owners working crazy hours, are unable to delegate, become control freaks, and the like.

Undermining Your Own Success

You might attribute your success to luck, timing, or external factors rather than your skills and hard work. This diminishes your achievements and feeds into the cycle of self-doubt. Hearing words like "Oh, Katie, I have just been lucky up until now" makes me cringe. Luck has a way of showing up after a truckload of effort has been put in! Luck to me is recognition of hard work.

Discounting Praise

When others compliment your work or achievements, you brush it off as them just being nice or not really understanding the situation. This prevents you from internalising positive feedback and building self-confidence. Next time someone pays you a compliment, just say, "Thank you."

Fear of Failure

The fear of making mistakes can paralyse you, preventing you from taking necessary risks and embracing new opportunities. This can stagnate growth and innovation in your clinic. Most decisions we see clinic owners make when we first start working with them is from a place of fear, rather than abundance. We are often so focused on what could go wrong, we forget to see what could go right.

A client of ours on the Elevate program at Thrive, who we'll call Harvey in this book, had a staff member who was not aligned with his company's values. Harvey had known this for a while, but because fear ruled his decisions, he had refrained from dealing with the problem. He feared what other people in the business would think because the staff member was likely to gossip, what hole this would leave in the business, what work he would have to pick up, the effort of recruiting and onboarding someone new, etc.

That is all absolutely true. I have been through all of that numerous times in my own clinic, too. But we stopped and I said, "Okay, what if we flipped our perspective to see other possibilities? If this staff member is let go, your team will see you step up as a bold, brilliant leader and have a whole new level of respect for you.

You get to showcase how you do things in your business while making a statement that those who do not align with your values are not people who will take your team to the next level. It provides an opportunity to systemise and put in new processes for the role, and doing the work during the vacancy will allow you to see what type of person is truly needed for it. Our 12-step hiring and recruiting process is simple and already laid out for you, so you can go hire someone who is world-class because that's what your business deserves." Guess what Harvey did? He had the conversation, of course.

How many times do you instantly think about what will go wrong instead of what could go brilliantly well? Or what you might learn? We simply decided to entertain a different way of thinking – you can do the same.

How to Overcome Imposter Syndrome

Overcoming imposter syndrome is not about eliminating self-doubt entirely. If anyone has mastered that, close this book and sail away into the sunset! It is about managing it effectively.

7/10 Rule

In the quest for excellence, many clinic owners find themselves paralysed by the pursuit of perfection. This is where the 7/10 rule becomes an invaluable tool. The principle behind the 7/10 rule is simple yet profound: Instead of striving for perfection, or a 10 out of 10, aim for a solid 7 out of 10. This mindset helps to overcome procrastination and self-doubt, ensuring that tasks are completed efficiently and effectively without being bogged down by unrealistic standards.

Allow yourself to produce work that is good enough to move forward, rather than getting stuck in an endless cycle of revisions and improvements that can lead to procrastination and burnout. Take a look at an example of this.

Perfectionist Approach: Delaying the launch of a marketing campaign until every single element is flawless, from the design to the copy.

7/10 Approach: Launch the campaign when it is well-designed and communicates your message effectively, even if there are a few minor imperfections. This enables you to start attracting patients sooner and allows for adjustments based on feedback and results.

Stop Comparing

When you first started your clinic, did you constantly compare your progress to that of the local competitors? Were you always scrutinising their social media, analysing their services, and measuring your success against theirs? This comparison trap often only fuels imposter syndrome, making us feel inadequate, overwhelmed, and chasing to be like someone else.

I did this too!

It is important to quickly realise that this habit is not only unhealthy, but also counterproductive. Focusing on what others are doing means you can lose sight of your own unique vision and goals. As President Theodore Roosevelt once said, "Comparison is the thief of joy."

How would you feel about going cold turkey and unfollowing your competitors online? Instead, shift your focus inward and concentrate on your clinic's strengths and the unique value you offer to clients.

By letting go of the need to compare, you will be able to cultivate a mindset of abundance rather than scarcity. Appreciate your journey and celebrate the milestones you have already achieved, no matter how small they seem in comparison to others. This shift in mindset will be liberating and instrumental in overcoming your imposter syndrome.

Acknowledge Your Feelings

The first step to overcoming imposter syndrome is recognising and acknowledging your feelings of self-doubt. Understand that these feelings are normal and experienced by many high achievers. I have it too, and it normally attacks when I am about to take the next big step

– like writing this book for example! Let me tell you, imposter syndrome could rule the show if I let it. I remember asking myself, "If I don't do this, then what impact would I end up making on our industry?" Right then and there I knew the answer was "Very small." So, I forged on and here we are!

Celebrate Your Achievements

It is so easy for us to focus on the one client we were not able to help get better, the one staff member we had a challenging time with that week or the 4,567 things we did not get done on our to-do list. Remembering the good things that happened too will help you greatly.

Every Friday in Team Thrive we share #fridaycheers. This can be one or however many things that you'd like to celebrate and share that week. Sharing what has gone well really allows you to shift your focus as the working week draws to a close. My husband and I do this over a glass of something too!

Build a Support Network

Surround yourself with supportive colleagues, mentors, and friends who understand your journey and can offer encouragement and advice. Did you know you are the average of the five people you spend the most time with?

And I probably should say at this point, get a coach! All great coaches are coached. It helps us work through self-doubt, imposter syndrome, confidence crisis and gives us that support and push that often we don't get from close ones. Not because they don't care, but because they don't really "get it." But your coach really gets it!

Embrace Who You Really Are

One of the most powerful antidotes to imposter syndrome is embracing your authentic self. Authenticity is about being true to who you are, both personally and professionally. It's about recognising and valuing your unique strengths, experiences, and perspectives.

When new members join our program one of the first things we do is get them to complete a colour and strengths test. This does a few things. First, we get to know them really well and really quickly, so we can support them and coach them in the way they need and will respond to best. Second, they get to see on paper how they are wired. It allows them to see why things in their business have felt so hard, where they need to spend more time, and how they can show up as their authentic selves in their business. And third, it allows them to start to cultivate their values, which are at the *root* of how everything happens in the business.

Create and Define Your Vision, Mission and Values

Creating and defining your vision, mission, and values is a foundational step in establishing a successful clinic. This will allow you to be more solid in your identity and help you push back whenever the imposter syndrome strikes.

Your vision is a forward-looking statement that articulates the long-term goals and aspirations for your clinic, painting a picture of what you hope to achieve in the future. The mission defines your clinic's core purpose and the specific, tangible ways you plan to achieve your vision. It serves as a roadmap for your day-to-day operations and decision-making processes.

Values are the guiding principles that shape your clinic's culture and inform how you interact with patients, staff, and the broader community. They reflect what is most important to you and your practice, such as integrity, compassion, excellence, and innovation.

Our values in my clinic are: Every ONE matters, Authentic, Empowering, and Exceptional.

In Thrive, this is how we do things: Be Bold, Be in Integrity, Be the 5%, Be You Always, Be Responsible.

Clearly articulating your vision, mission, and values is crucial because it aligns your team, fosters a sense of purpose, and drives consistent action toward achieving your goals. It also helps to build trust and loyalty among clients and staff by demonstrating a commitment to a higher standard of care and service.

When everyone in your clinic understands and embraces these guiding statements, it creates a cohesive, motivated, and focused team dedicated to making your clinic a success. Take out your journal and note down your values personally and within your business. If these don't quickly roll off the tongue, this is something I would encourage you to get help to work on. They are the lifeblood of your clinic. Team management, leadership, and decision-making all become clearer when we have these in place.

Our next chapters will move on to the trunk of the tree now that we have laid down some foundations. Remember the trunk cannot grow without solid, healthy roots that need watering and feeding often; it is not set and forget!

By acknowledging and managing imposter syndrome, you can foster an environment that supports your vision and empowers you to lead confidently. Reflect on your values and achievements, setting the stage for further growth and success.

But, as you move forward, keep in mind that overcoming imposter syndrome is an ongoing process. There will be moments of doubt and insecurity, but with the right mindset and support, you can navigate these challenges and continue to grow both personally and professionally.

4

Pruning the Overgrowth

You started this business because you're passionate about what you do. You care deeply about improving the health and wellness of your clients. Some of you may have fallen into this role, some may have needed to get out of the NHS, while some may have always dreamt of being in this industry.

As we start our business, it evolves and grows naturally much like a little seed in the ground. I see lots of owners from before 2020 whose businesses are going great thanks to their excellent reputation. They're really good physios, osteopaths, or sports therapists, and word-of-mouth has helped their business grow organically.

If that sounds like you, then here's likely what happened. You jumped onto this crazy hamster wheel and started seeing more and more patients. You started opening your diary up more and ended up doing clinical hours over six days a week, seeing around 60 patients. Then you started having to invoice insurance companies, send more emails, create more rehab programmes and treatment plans, and generally just became so much busier. The hamster wheel spun quicker and quicker and quicker and quicker. Before you knew it, you'd created an out-of-control tree that is overgrown, uncontrollable, and much like Japanese knotweed, a pain in the ass!

We can't get in control and we just end up madly trying to fight fires. Well, guess what? It usually takes three years to treat Japanese knotweed!

The reason for this hamster wheel and Japanese knotweed hybrid is likely because of a lack of a clear plan, strategy, and set of goals from the very beginning of the business. The clarity around the "why" was not there, nor was the vision; not a vision of "owning a big clinic, with an MDT service" but a vision that is driven by numbers.

Another analogy I use to help clinic owners see the importance of having a plan is this: Imagine you are driving from Sheffield to somewhere in Scotland without a sat nav, or a map if you're still old-school. This is exactly like running a business without a plan. It would take you *ages* to get there. In fact, I would never make it! You will go round and round in circles, it will cost a fortune in fuel and time and the destination is not clear anyway, so when you do get to that somewhere, you won't even know you've arrived!

Taking a step back to reconnect with the why is imperative to clinic success. Otherwise, you can end up creating something that is not what you wanted or what you set out to do. I can't imagine anyone would ever plant a Japanese knotweed on purpose.

Taking a Strategic Pause

It's crucial to take time away from daily operations to focus on the bigger picture.

In Thrive, we set out a day for our clinic owners to come to an in-person event that allows them to step back and evaluate their business from an external perspective. This dedicated time for strategic thinking and planning is a game-changer. Getting out of your business for a full day quarterly is something I would highly recommend. I call it a "Thrive clarity day." If that feels too much right now, try once annually to set a plan for the next year, and then half yearly to check in and reset again.

For many clinic owners, the biggest hurdle to taking this pause is the fear of losing revenue or disappointing clients. However, short-term sacrifices are often necessary for long-term gains. By reallocating time from immediate client care to strategic planning, clinic owners can identify areas where their business is losing money and find opportunities for growth.

In my own practice, we typically take an entire day to develop our growth plan for the upcoming financial year. We analyse what had worked well in the past and identify areas for improvement. I recall one year when this exercise revealed opportunities to increase revenue by £300,000 without expanding our team or increasing overhead costs. This kind of insight is invaluable and only possible when we take the time to step back and evaluate our business from a strategic standpoint. If we had instead worked at the clinic that day we did our session, we would have made only £1,500 gross revenue!

The Importance of a Growth Plan

Creating a growth plan begins with understanding the why behind your business. This foundational element shapes your financial projections, strategic decisions like when to hire and who to hire first, when to price rise, and ultimately ensures that your business serves you, providing the income, time, and fulfilment you desire.

It's about asking, "Why don't I get a normal job?" and clarifying what truly drives you to keep running your business.

There is no time like now. Take out your journal and ask yourself these questions.

Why don't I get a normal job?

Why are you running your own business?

What drives you to get up every day and just keep going?

What is important to you (freedom and flexibility, financial security, time with family, etc.)?

I want you to wake up every day, every week, and every month and know what you are aiming for, what you are working for, what your targets are, and all that. This may feel intense to some of you, but without it, you lose focus and direction; you say yes to things that don't serve you in moving towards your goal and you end up being a busy fool.

As a high achiever and a recovering people pleaser, I often catch myself getting back onto the hamster wheel. Sometimes I catch myself early enough, sometimes I don't. But I am getting better every day and every week at saying *no* to things that don't bring me joy, align with my goals and are not in my zone of genius. But this can only happen when you *stop*, get out of your business and spend time mapping out what the next 12 months look like for you.

Some of you will be able to go for 3, 5, 10 years! I admire your brain.

The one thing which is important to add is that if you're thinking about selling your business down the line, you need to plan when. If it's within 5 years, the entire plan should be about ensuring the business is built to sell, meaning that you will need to be able to get out of the day-to-day operations.

When you are clear on why and what your vision is for this business, we have to create your strategic plan, and then add the numbers to it.

Your business *must* be profitable. Period.

With profits, you can impact your community, your family, and your friends on a much bigger scale. You can hire great team members; you can add services and you can live your Level 10 life!

Many clinic owners tell me they are not in it for the money, and I call BS on that. I have never heard that from a clinic owner who is actually making loads either.

Be okay with the fact that you are in it for the money. Money makes the world go round! Money is a byproduct of you running an efficient, systemised, streamlined, and impactful business. So, if you are not in it for the money, I really hope you are already loaded and just doing this out of the goodness of your own heart in your free time.

To create a business that truly serves you, it's essential to align every aspect of your operation with your vision. This means being intentional about how you spend your time, making strategic decisions that drive growth, and ensuring that profit is a priority baked into every transaction.

Start by revisiting your business's foundational elements. Is the original "why" still relevant, or has it evolved over time? Does your current business model support your lifestyle and priorities? Your business should facilitate your life, not the other way around. Remember, going into business without a plan is like embarking on a journey without a map.

In the next chapter, we will look at how to create your growth plan for your clinic and take home more money, rather than feeling like the lowest-paid employee. Does this sound good? I invite you to turn the page.

5

Strengthening the Trunk

In the previous chapter, we looked at the "why," so hopefully you have now reconnected with why you are running this business and how it needs to serve you.

Transitioning from feeling like you have a job to a business requires a master plan that has a solid financial strategy linked to it. This is often one of the two missing links when we chat with clinic owners. They just don't have a plan – which is the trunk of the tree!

Developing a Step-by-Step Growth Plan

In this chapter, we'll explore how to develop a step-by-step growth plan and how to use the Profit First accounting method to increase your take-home pay. Sounds good, right?

Starting With the End in Mind

To chart your path from A to B, start by envisioning what B looks like. What is your ultimate goal for your clinic? This vision could be about achieving a certain level of financial success, expanding your services, or building a legacy.

Clearly defining this endpoint will allow you to guide your strategic decisions and keep you focused on your journey.

I think it's important at this point to say that your business needs to feed you, so your end goals and subgoals definitely need to include your take-home pay. You should never be the poorest paid person in your own business. This is unless of course you are very new in business or are reinvesting heavily. However, this will wear thin quickly, trust me!

Breaking Down the Vision

Once your end goal is clear, break it down into achievable milestones.

If we think about 12 months from now, what would you like to be celebrating if we were chatting over a glass of champagne? Maybe it's that you are now working two days clinically, but revenue and profit have remained the same. Maybe it's that you are consistently taking home £4,000 per month. Maybe it's that you have hired a practice administrator and are no longer doing all the billing, invoicing, and bookings for the clinic. Maybe you have taken six weeks of holidays completely unplugged!

Now, let's take that goal and reverse engineer it.

Let's take the goal of taking £4,000 take-home income as an example, and let's assume you are taking £2,000 now. You can plot the increase from £2,000 to £4,000 over 12 months.

I would always encourage you to not set a revenue goal first! This is a secondary goal based on the profit and take-home you want.

Many clinic owners mistakenly focus solely on increasing revenue, believing that more money will solve their problems. However, revenue is just a vanity metric.

True success lies in understanding and maximising profit. This involves analysing the cost of delivery, operational overheads, and other expenses to ensure that the business is financially sustainable.

Identifying Key Strategies

Being able to identify key strategies is simply reverse engineering where you want to be to where you are now. I call this the 1,3,5 plan. Below is an example of this in action.

One Goal:

- Hit £4,000 take-home income and have three evenings at home a week.

From here, we think of the strategies we can take towards the goal.

Three Key Strategies:

- Review prices and a possible increase
- Introduce new programs and packages to improve conversion rate and retention rate
- Hire an evening physiotherapist

From here, we can then think about the tactics we will deploy to achieve these three objectives.

Five Tactics:

- Put new prices into projections to see what impact that has on profit before deciding on how much to increase by
- Set increased pricing for every follow-up session by 1st November
- Prepare a letter for the clients to hand out by 15th September
- Create an in-house poster to explain there is a price increase starting 1st November
- Hand out a letter by 1st October (giving four weeks' notice)

By doing it this way, we have reverse-engineered the goal and created an easy starting point.

You can see that the list of five above are what we call "tactics." But you cannot focus on the tactics first, as this will invariably lead to being very busy but not moving forward, spending time on things that are not moving you towards your goal, and in fact bringing you further away from it and eventually toward burnout and exhaustion.

Focusing on the tactics, or the branches, first will ultimately lead to burnout or exhaustion, wanting to quit, sleepless nights, not being present at home, feeling like you're spinning a million plates, not making the money you want to make, wasting money on marketing that doesn't work, spending more money on CPD courses that have no returns, hiring team members who turn out to be a pain in the ass and all that. Do any of these sound familiar? I thought so!

Monitoring and Adjusting

A growth plan isn't static; it needs regular review and adjustments. Set up quarterly reviews to assess your progress, celebrate wins, and identify areas for improvement. Even if you run a clinic by yourself, book a meeting with yourself now in the diary, otherwise 12 months fly by and it's too late to adjust your course.

If a strategy isn't working as expected, be prepared to pivot and try something new.

Take Home More Money With the Profit First Method

One of the things that really gets on my wick is how little clinic owners pay themselves. I speak to hundreds of clinic owners every year and I can count on one hand how many times I've thought, "Great, they are taking a decent salary for the effort and risk they have." So why is this?

We covered a lot of the reasons in previous chapters. There are the beliefs around self-worth, your money thermostat, and even the persistent "What will people think of me?!" question niggling in their minds. Apart from these, the main reason I see is that clinic owners do not prioritise profit.

Traditional accounting often puts profit last:

Revenue - Expenses = Profit

The Profit First method flips this equation:

Revenue - Profit = Expenses

This approach prioritises profit by setting it aside first, forcing you to operate within the remaining budget.

Profit First has personally transformed my businesses for the better, so if it works for me, it will work for you!

I can and will take zero credit for this. It is the work of American entrepreneur and author Mike Michalowicz. I am sure he will never read this book, but in the true sense of manifestation, if you do, Mike, I would love to co-author a book with you!

Mike says "Profit is not an event.[2]" I love this for a few reasons, let me explain.

If you are waiting until your accountant sends you your year-end P&L, which will or will not show how much profit you made that year, then you are treating profit like an event.

You will also look around at that point and wonder where the heck that profit actually is – because it's likely not showing up in your bank account.

Five Rules for the Profit First Method

Rule One. Profit needs to be baked into every transaction in your business. It is a habit! Your job as the clinic owner is to find ways to maximise profit. Don't wait until the end of year to see that you have not made a bean.

Rule Two. Do not think you need to grow first and then you will find profit in the process. That is a backwards way to think.

Rule Three. You cannot outgrow a profit problem. This is something I see a lot of clinic owners do. They think hiring another self-employed associate who takes 50% commission is their route to success and more money. Good luck!

Rule Four. If it is not making a profit, saving money or saving you time, dump it. When you focus on growth, you scramble to grow – often at all costs, inevitably including your health. When you focus on profit first, you figure out how to grow without losing your sanity along the way.

Rule Five. Stop checking your bank account! If you are using this as a measure of how well your business is or is not doing, stop. You need an effective money management system.

All these rules ultimately lead us to your financial strategy. Profit must come first. From this point we can work out how to run a lean business, what revenue your company can generate with the current team you have, the optimal pricing structure, and what operational hours you should have.

It becomes obvious then when you need to implement tactics such as raising your prices, bringing on another team member, and fixing the holes in the sales funnel, to name a few.

A Clear Path Forward

Transitioning from a reactive, day-to-day clinic operation to a strategic, growth-focused business requires clarity, discipline, and the right tools. By developing a step-by-step growth plan and implementing the Profit First method, you can ensure your clinic not only survives but thrives.

One of our Activate members, who we'll call Jane, was in a bit of chaos prior to joining our program. Her numbers were all over the show, expenses were too high due to their staffing model and a ridiculous commission structure, she had an inconsistent take-home pay, and she owed the business money as she was taking out more than it was earning. Imagine the sleepless nights, high levels of stress, and the desire to simply bury her head in the sand. We went through her finances with her and set out the Profit First accounting model.

She now has a streamlined, operationally tight business, she takes out a regularly increasing monthly income, she has her tax money accounted for, and even has separate pots for operating expenses, profit, tax, and wages. Cue her feeling confident and managing her money well, therefore giving the signals she is ready to receive more. The business is growing a solid trunk and roots system.

Remember, this journey is uniquely yours. Stay committed to your vision, make strategic decisions based on your goals, and prioritise profit along the way. As you do, you'll find that reaching your destination isn't just about the destination itself but about building a sustainable, rewarding business that serves you and your community. At this point, most clinic owners may feel overwhelmed and not really sure where to start. I hope you will give me permission at this point to offer my help. I see it as having two options.

You can figure it out for yourself, which will take a lot of time as you don't currently have the knowledge. It will cost a lot of money too, not just in terms of cost but also from you using up time you could be spending making a profit.

Or you could reach out for a discovery call with my team. We understand first-hand the value of talking through your clinic's situation with someone who has walked that path before you, especially when it comes to creating an actionable plan to overcome any obstacles to success. You don't need to do this alone. In fact, that to me is insanity.

When I was young, I wanted to learn the piano so I got a piano teacher – the wonderfully kind and patient Mrs. Cherry. When I was older, I wanted to get better at badminton, so I got a coach. When I was older still, I wanted to get better at the "business side" of running my clinic, so I got a coach! Am I making my point? Successful people ask themselves, "Who do I need?" and not "How do I do it?" Now, it's the time you have all been waiting for. It's time for tactics!

Thank you for being patient and giving these chapters the time they deserve. I am confident that if you have read all the previous chapters and done the work, you are ready to fix the branches of that tree. The first one is the money branch. Excited? You should be.

6

Bringing the Money Branch to Life

We have now put down the essential roots of mindset and built a sturdy trunk with your master plan. It's now time to grow the first vital branch: Money, a.k.a. sales!

A few things will happen when you start reading this chapter. You may flick through it thinking, "I hate the word 'sales.' I'll just skim this section and find the bit about marketing, that's what I really need." Or you will find out that this may be the biggest hole in your business right now and you hadn't realised it!

Why Your Sales Funnel Must Come First

Without a strong sales funnel, all the marketing in the world won't yield the results you're aiming for. Marketing brings people to your door, but your sales funnel is what brings them into your clinic, keeps them coming back and ultimately drives your success.

Imagine you've launched an impressive marketing campaign and the phone is ringing off the hook. Great, right? But what if the enquiries don't convert into appointments? Or worse, what if those initial appointments don't lead to long-term clients?

This is where the sales funnel comes in. It's the process that turns prospects into clients and then into loyal clients. If your funnel is leaky, you'll be losing potential business at every stage. Fixing your sales funnel first ensures that when your marketing brings people in, they actually stick around and you're not burning through your cash.

Think of your sales funnel as the backbone of your business. It doesn't just influence the initial transaction; it shapes the entire client experience. From the first contact to ongoing treatment plans, a well-structured funnel can mean the difference between a clinic that's thriving and one that's just surviving.

The Key to Conversion: The Consultative Selling Method

A key part of any successful sales funnel is your conversion rate – the percentage of prospects who turn into paying clients. To maximise this, you need a strategy that builds trust and demonstrates value right from the start.

This is where the Consultative Selling Method comes in. Unlike traditional sales approaches, which can feel pushy or impersonal, consultative selling is all about building relationships and offering solutions that meet your patients' needs.

Let's break down the five essential components of this method.

Rapport

The foundation of any successful patient relationship is rapport. People do business with those they like and trust. From the moment a potential patient walks through your door or picks up the phone, your goal should be to make them feel comfortable and valued. This might seem simple, but it's crucial. A warm smile, active listening, and genuine interest in their well-being can make all the difference.

This is about you taking the lead and instilling confidence that they are in the right place and that you are there to help them.

Framing

Once you've established rapport, it's time to frame the conversation. This is the most important step that most miss out on. This means setting the stage for what the client can expect during their visit with you, and most importantly explaining that if you are the right person to help them, you will tell them what that partnership will look like at the end of the session.

For example, you might say, "Today, I'm going to ask you a few questions to better understand your condition and goals. Then, I'll explain how we can help you achieve those goals with a personalised treatment plan."

This not only sets expectations but also positions you as a professional who is focused on their specific needs.

It holds you accountable to having that clear conversation with them at the end. This also allows you to lead and not be led, a.k.a. the client is stripping off as they walk through the door!

State A

"State A" refers to the client's current situation - the pain points or challenges that brought them to your clinic in the first place. During this stage, your role is to help the client articulate what's bothering them.

Use probing questions to dig deeper into their issues, and listen carefully to their answers. This is also known as the subjective assessment, but what we often miss out on here is the emotional connection.

People buy themselves out of a problem and into a solution. They are not buying physio sessions, k-taping or joint mobilisations! So, we must go below the surface and try and get them to verbalise what impact this problem is having on their life.

It's important to let the client express their concerns fully. This not only helps you understand their needs but also allows the patient to feel heard and understood. By the end of this stage, you should have a clear picture of where the client is currently and what they're struggling with.

State B

"State B" is the ideal outcome – the goal that the client wants to achieve. This is where you paint a picture of what their life could look like after receiving treatment. It's about helping them see the potential benefits of working with you and how their condition could improve.

For instance, you might say, "Imagine being able to play with your kids without worrying about back pain," or "Think about how great it would feel to wake up in the morning without stiffness in your neck."

By contrasting State A with State B, you create a sense of urgency and motivation for the client to take action. You also show the gap between where they are now and where they want to be.

At this point, you may move into your objective assessment to continue to find out more, offer that diagnosis or prognosis and have a more thorough plan of how you are going to work with them.

Recap & Close

After guiding the client through their current challenges and potential future outcomes, it's time to recap and close the sale. The recap is a summary of what you've discussed, including their pain points and the solutions you can offer.

For example, you might say, "So, if I'm hearing you correctly, you're struggling with [pain point], and it's affecting your [daily activity]. What we can do is [a treatment plan] to help you achieve [State B]." This recap reinforces the value you're offering and ensures that you and the patient are on the same page.

Finally, you move to the close. The close isn't about hard selling; it's about asking for a commitment. You might say, "How does that sound to you?" or "Are you ready to start your journey to recovery with us?"

By this point, if you've built rapport, framed the conversation correctly, and clearly shown the benefits of moving from State A to State B, the client should feel confident and ready to move forward.

If you are reading this and your conversion rate is not at 75% or above, you need to work on this first! In my clinic, our conversion rate is set at 85% as standard, because we believe 85% of all patients who walk through our doors would benefit from seeing us again.

What is your conversion rate sitting at and what is your target?

The Importance of Retention Rate

Conversion is just the beginning. Once you've turned a prospect into a client, the next challenge is to keep them coming back. This is where your retention rate comes into play.

Retention is critical because acquiring a new patient can cost up to five times more than retaining an existing one. Moreover, loyal clients are more likely to refer others to your clinic, providing a steady stream of new business without additional marketing costs.

So, how do you improve retention in your clinic? Here are a few strategies.

Go to the Subscription Route

Stop offering PAYG and bring programs of treatment or subscriptions into your clinic. If you can't fix a client's problem in one session, why do we only run PAYG? Clients want the fastest possible solution to their pain or injury.

WeightWatchers, Slimming World, and all other reputable companies like this and personal trainers exist because people need accountability. They need ongoing support to prioritise their health and wellness.

Life is busy for everyone, and remembering to do your exercises and keep doing them even when things start to improve is hard! So, we need to create a structure that supports our clients to achieve their optimum health.

Consistent Follow-Up

Regular follow-ups show that you care about your clients' progress. Whether it's a quick phone call after their first appointment or a reminder text for their next session, consistent communication helps build a strong relationship and keeps clients engaged with their treatment plan. Look at your touch points for your clients, what could improve there?

You could introduce a standard into your practice so that all patients have either one of three expected outcomes: They either rebook, schedule another follow-up phone call, or are discharged. This ensures the words "We'll see how it goes" are never uttered!

Acquiring clients costs money and servicing those clients costs money, so being really clear on your conversion rate and retention rate expectations in your clinic is the route to making more money quickly.

Exceptional Customer Service

Never underestimate the power of great customer service. From the first interaction to every follow-up visit, make sure your team is providing a warm, welcoming and professional experience. A friendly receptionist, a clean and comfortable environment, and staff who go the extra mile can turn a one-time visitor into a loyal patient.

And I have to add here, please weed the front of your clinics. Even better, pay someone to weed for you. First impressions really count!

Loyalty Programs

Consider implementing a loyalty program to reward your regular patients. This could be in the form of added value, a small gift, or a voucher to try another service within your clinic. Loyalty programs not only incentivise repeat visits but also make patients feel appreciated.

Shifting Your Business Model and Mindset

At this point in your business, it's likely impossible for you to grow exponentially. Could you handle ten times the clients tomorrow?

My guess is no! How you deliver your work to clients matters more than you might think, and we have all become stuck in exchanging time for money.

Your current business model cannot be scaled exponentially because it relies heavily on people. You can definitely get more customers, yes, but PAYG models which we have seen in clinics since their inception are now outdated!

By keeping your existing business model the same, we are depriving countless people of your beneficial solutions. Right now, it's likely that you feel trapped in the churn of patients. What you may not know is that there are countless permutations for how you could deliver your solutions and services in a beneficial way, without having all the results or delivery depend on you and your thumbs!

A belief like "Anything new wouldn't work" is something called a sacred cow. A belief you hold as untouchable and unchangeable, even though it's just a belief, and beliefs can be changed.

These deeply rooted beliefs of their only being one way to deliver a service – usually, the way it's always been done, and sometimes yes, for good reason – are simply not true, no matter what industry. In my opinion, we have a lot of sacred cows within our industry.

When there is a will, there is always a way, especially when we allow ourselves to be creative. This requires us to look at the roots again, have a willingness to see things differently and to try a different approach.

To help expand your thinking, you can try asking yourself the following questions:

- What would need to shift in my business for my clinic to provide our services to ten times the number of clients we work with now?
- How could I remove myself from all of our most of the delivery and replace myself?
- What would be the best solution for our customers and their problems?

One of our Elevate clients had been an osteopath for more than 30 years when he came on board with us, and so the belief that "This is the way it's always been done" was a strong one for him.

Our first plan of action for him was to shift the business model away from PAYG and into treatment programs, plus a price rise. This was essential to drive more profit and improve the retention rate.

In the first two months, he doubled his income and managed to take a full week off! If someone who has done it a certain way for more than three decades can pivot and adapt to changes, there is nothing stopping you.

As you cultivate the sales branch of your clinic, it's essential to remember not to means-test your clients when recommending next steps. Your responsibility as a healthcare provider is to offer the best possible treatment plan based on their needs, not their perceived financial situation. Assume your clients want the best care and are willing to invest in their health.

By doing so, you ensure that you're providing the most effective solutions without unconsciously limiting their options. Trust in the value of your services and in your clients' commitment to their well-being, and you'll create a more robust, ethical, and successful clinic.

7

Branching Out

On our journey through the Clinic Success Tree, we've explored the roots that ground your clinic, the trunk that supports its growth, and the vital sales branch. Now, it's time to delve into the one I know you've all been waiting for, the branch that feeds the lifeblood of your clinic: Marketing.

This chapter is dedicated to helping you understand how to connect with the right audience, those who genuinely need your services and will benefit most from your expertise and make you visible. The first thing I would like you to remember is that visibility is currency. To generate revenue and profit you must be visible. There is no clinic that can hide under a rock and make money - that's impossible! I know lots of clinic owners tell me they hate having to sell their soul on social media and there seems to be a lot of worry about "being called out" in the industry. But I want to reassure you that you can be visible in a way that is authentic and aligns with you and your values. So where do you start when it comes to marketing? Flyers, Facebook, doing a TikTok dance?

…No!

Figuring It Out: Clients, Services and Messaging

Imagine standing outside your clinic, watching a line of 100 people with back pain waiting to see you. Among these people, only a small percentage - around 5% - would immediately recognise that you, as a physiotherapist or an osteopath, are the professional they need to help solve their problem. The other 95% might be thinking about consulting Dr. Google, trying some YouTube exercises or visiting their GP for pain relief. It's startling, isn't it? As health professionals, we often assume that everyone understands what we do and how we can help. But the truth is, most people don't. They aren't aware that a physiotherapist could be the answer to their problems.

I am sure most people think I run onto a rugby pitch with a bucket of water and a sponge when I say I'm a physio!

This lack of awareness is a significant challenge but also an enormous opportunity. It's why defining your "who" – your ideal client – is so critical in your marketing strategy. If you try to be everything to everybody, you end up being nothing to nobody. Your marketing needs to resonate with the specific people you can help, rather than broadcasting a general message that fails to connect with anyone.

To effectively market your clinic, you need to step into your client's shoes and view the world through their eyes. Imagine peering through the keyhole of their lives and understanding not just their physical pain but the ripple effects that pain has on their daily existence. Let's take the example of a footballer with a knee injury. Beyond the physical pain, this individual might be worried about missing training, losing fitness, or even jeopardising their career. Their concern isn't just the knee. It's the impact on their income, their ability to provide for their family and their future in the sport they love.

Or let's take a mum of two who has no time to herself, has been struggling with back pain since pregnancy, and is struggling to lean over the cot and lift her baby out. She is sleep-deprived, and when she can get some shuteye, her back pain keeps her awake. She has a short fuse with her toddler and spends most of the days in a fog of pain and sleep deprivation.

This deeper understanding of your client's problems will allow your marketing to stand out. It's not enough to say, "I treat knee injuries." Instead, you should communicate that you help athletes return to their peak performance, regain their confidence, and secure their livelihoods. Or that you work with women who need to be pain-free to enjoy their children without distraction. When you can speak to the broader impact of their pain or injury, you'll find that your message resonates much more powerfully with those who need your services.

Another factor to consider is your services. What do you offer? Is everything and anything on the table? Many clinic owners resist niching down because they fear losing potential clients. It's a common concern: "If I specialise, won't I miss out on all the other people I could be helping?" But in reality, the opposite is true. By trying to cater to everyone, your message becomes diluted, and you struggle to attract anyone at all.

Think about your practice for a moment. If you had to choose just one type of client or one type of problem to focus on, who would it be? Perhaps it's women going through menopause and struggling with pain, stiffness and soreness, or maybe it's athletes recovering from injuries. Whoever it is, by becoming an expert in that area, you not only stand out from the competition but you also make it easier for your ideal clients to find you. They will recognise you as the specialist who truly understands their unique challenges and can offer the solutions they need.

Caveat warning! If you run a multidisciplinary clinic, you absolutely can have different professionals and multiple different ideal clients, but - and it's a big *but* - when it comes to marketing, you should have one ideal client per campaign.

One of the biggest mistakes clinic owners make is focusing their marketing on what they do rather than how they help. Listing your services - physiotherapy, sports massage, dry needling - might make sense to you, but it's unlikely to resonate with potential clients. They don't care about the specific techniques you use; they care about the results you can achieve for them. Consider the language you use in your marketing materials. Instead of talking about the services you offer, shift the focus to the problems you solve. For example, instead of saying, "We offer physiotherapy sessions," you might say, "We help busy professionals relieve back pain so they can get back to doing what they love." This approach speaks directly to the needs and desires of your target audience and makes it clear that you understand their pain points and know how to address them.

When you specialise in a particular niche, you create a market of one – a unique space where you are the go-to expert. This doesn't mean you can't have multiple specialties, but each one should be marketed separately. For example, if you specialise in treating menopausal women and in treating sports injuries, both should have their own marketing campaign that speaks directly to the specific needs of those audiences.

Each campaign should be tailored to the distinct problems and concerns of the group you're targeting. This way, when someone from that group comes across your marketing, they immediately see that you understand their situation and are the right person to help them. Whether it's a menopausal woman struggling with joint pain or an athlete worried about getting back on the field, your message should speak directly to them.

As you look around your community, you'll notice that many people could benefit from your services – whether it's the person hobbling through the grocery store or the colleague complaining about shoulder pain. There is no shortage of demand for what you offer. Yet many clinics struggle to attract the clients they need to thrive. Why is that? Often, it comes down to how you're positioning your services. If you're too focused on promoting your profession – "I'm a physiotherapist" – instead of the solutions you provide, you're missing out on opportunities. The demand is there, but your potential clients don't realise that you are the one who can help them because your marketing isn't connecting with their specific needs, *or* you are just not visible (a.k.a. you are not doing any marketing consistently!).

To change this, start thinking about your marketing as a conversation with your ideal client. What are they worried about? What are their goals? How can you alleviate their pain and help them achieve what they want? When you can answer these questions clearly and compellingly, you'll find that clients begin to seek you out because they recognise that you understand them and can help them.

Being Visible: The Whys and Hows

One of the most common mistakes clinic owners make is underestimating the power of consistent visibility. You might think that because you've placed a flyer in a coffee shop or posted on social media once, your job is done. However, visibility isn't a one-and-done task. It's about being present consistently and across multiple channels so that when someone needs your services, your name is the first one that comes to mind. There are three main things to remember as you go about your marketing.

Diversify your touchpoints. Don't rely on a single marketing channel. Use a combination of Google Ads, social media, local events, sponsorships, and collaborations. This multi-layered approach ensures that your clinic is visible in different places, reaching clients where they are most likely to see you. And always think that where your ideal clients are hanging out is where you need to be!

Track and measure. It's not enough to be visible; you need to know what's working. Track where your leads are coming from and which marketing efforts are bringing in the most clients. This allows you to focus on the strategies that are effective and refine those that aren't.

Be consistent. Ensure your messaging is consistent across all platforms. Whether it's a flyer, a social media post, or a Google Ad, your message should clearly communicate who you help. Avoid jargon and focus on addressing the specific pain points of your ideal clients. If you write marketing copy in medical terms, people will not resonate with it, and they will take no action.

The idea that people need to see your message multiple times before taking action isn't just a marketing myth - it's a fundamental principle. Your goal should be to ensure that your clinic is visible in at least seven different ways to your potential clients.

This might include:

- Google Ads
- Social Media
- Local Sponsorships
- Flyers and Posters
- Email Marketing
- Word of Mouth
- Workshops

Each of these methods increases the likelihood that when someone thinks of needing your services, they think of your clinic first. Note that I suggest not making social media your biggest priority as there are far better ways to generate leads on other platforms. And remember, if you have an audience of 1,000, you are probably getting less than 10 people engaging with your posts!

Your clinic's success is directly tied to how visible you are to your potential clients. This means not only maintaining your current visibility but constantly looking for new ways to increase it.

I recall in May 2024, I was abroad, staying in a gorgeous hotel, and I received a message to let me know the website was down for my clinic and no one knew what to do! I am going to cut this story short as your time is money, but after six hours of talking to a chatbot and to someone in the company who owns my domain name – who also advised I spend £400 to fix the problem (which I did, as at this point I had lost all sight of other possible solutions) – and finally to my website hosts who eventually saved the day, we were finally close to being back online. At that point, the website had actually been down for three days.

When a situation like this ever happens in my business my first thought, apart from cursing, of course, are questions like, "Why is this being sent to me? What do I need to pay attention to?" There is a lesson in everything.

If you rely heavily on Google Ads and your website suddenly goes down, your client flow could be severely impacted. However, if you've built a diverse, multi-channel marketing strategy, a temporary issue like this won't cripple your business. Luckily it made very little impact on my business and profit, but for clinic owners who have nothing else in their marketing strategy, this is a problem!

Tactics for Effective Online Marketing: Three Essential Strategies

In the previous section, we discussed the importance of defining your ideal client and understanding their specific needs. Now, let's explore three practical marketing tactics that can significantly enhance your clinic's visibility and effectiveness. These strategies are essential for ensuring that your marketing efforts resonate with your target audience and translate into real results.

1. Maximise Your Visibility with Google My Business

For any local business, including clinics like yours and mine, visibility is crucial. One of the most effective and cost-efficient ways to achieve this is by leveraging Google My

Business (GMB). When someone searches for services like yours – "best physio in [your location]" – your GMB profile is often the first thing they'll see. This makes it a powerful tool for attracting potential clients who are already searching for the solutions you provide. Here are some simple pointers to optimising your Google My Business profile.

Complete every section thoroughly. Ensure that all sections of your profile are fully filled out, including your clinic's name, address, phone number, business hours, services and any relevant attributes (e.g. wheelchair accessibility). Consistency across your GMB profile, website and other directories improves credibility and helps with Google ranking.

Encourage and respond to client reviews. Actively ask clients for detailed reviews that mention your clinic's services and location. Reviews that include keywords like "physiotherapy" or "Pilates in [your location]" can boost your search ranking. Be sure to respond to all reviews – positive or negative – to show engagement and improve client trust.

Add fresh photos regularly. Update your profile with new, high-quality photos of your clinic, staff, and facilities.

Google favours active profiles, so adding photos of the team, treatment rooms or clinic events every quarter helps keep your listing fresh and engaging for potential clients.

By investing time in your GMB profile, you'll enhance your clinic's visibility, making it easier for potential clients to find and choose you over competitors. And please remember this is a part of your digital marketing strategy. It cannot be the only thing you do to enhance your visibility.

2. Personalise Your Marketing

People connect with people, not businesses. One of the most overlooked yet effective tactics in marketing is to showcase the faces behind your clinic. This humanises your brand and builds trust, which is essential when clients are choosing a healthcare provider. People buy from people.

You can implement this strategy in simple and practical ways like putting team photos on your website. Display clear, welcoming photos of your team on your website. Avoid generic headshots; instead, opt for images that show personality and warmth. Potential clients want to see who they'll be working with and feel reassured by a friendly, approachable team.

You can also engage with people on social media. Use platforms like Instagram and Facebook to share more about the people behind your clinic. Post photos of team activities, personal stories, and even everyday moments that showcase your clinic's culture. Content that features real people tends to generate higher engagement and builds stronger connections with your audience. By making your team visible and relatable, you're not just promoting your services – you're building relationships. Clients are more likely to choose a clinic where they feel a personal connection with the staff.

3. Invest in Paid Advertising

While free marketing tactics are valuable, investing in paid advertising is crucial for sustained growth and consistency in client acquisition. However, it's important to spend wisely and ensure that every pound you invest delivers measurable results. Here are key considerations when it comes to paid advertising.

Start with Google Ads. Google Ads are particularly effective for clinics because they target users actively searching for specific services. Set up campaigns that focus on the conditions you treat and the services you offer. For example, ads targeting "back pain treatment in [your location]" can directly attract potential clients with that specific need.

Track your ROI. Don't just spend money – measure the impact. Use tools to track how many clients your ads are bringing in, and adjust your strategy accordingly. This ensures that your advertising budget is spent efficiently and effectively. Do *not* engage with marketing companies until you know your exact cost per lead and your average client value.

Don't be afraid to spend. Many clinic owners are hesitant to invest in marketing, but not spending enough can lead to missed opportunities and being outpaced by competitors. A good benchmark is to allocate a consistent percentage of your revenue to marketing.

Paid advertising is a powerful way to gain control over your client flow, ensuring steady growth and reducing reliance on unpredictable word-of-mouth referrals. A caveat: I note that you must take into account not just the how, but the who as well. This is a prime example. If you are an expert in Google Ads, by all means, you can do this yourself. If you are not, find a company that can do this for you. I recommend people who are experts at working with clinic owners and can measure and track the results monthly for you. But you need to know what you're aiming for and what your average client value is. You are ultimately responsible for really understanding what return on investment you are getting.

A Healthy Marketing Branch: What You Need to Remember

Visibility is currency. Your clinic's success is directly linked to how visible you are to potential clients. Being visible consistently across multiple channels is crucial for attracting and retaining clients.

Define your ideal client. Understanding who your ideal client is and what their specific pain points are allows you to craft a marketing message that resonates. Don't try to be everything to everyone – focus on the clients you can help the most.

Move beyond fear to niche down. Specialising in a specific type of client or problem can help you stand out in a crowded market. Niching down doesn't mean losing potential clients, it means attracting the right ones who truly need your services.

Craft your message around pain and solutions. Shift your marketing focus from what you do to how you help. Clients are more interested in the results you can provide than the specific techniques you use. Speak to their problems and how you can solve them.

Optimise your Google My Business profile. A fully optimised GMB profile is essential for local visibility. Ensure your profile is complete, regularly updated with photos, and includes client reviews.

Showcase your team. Personalise your marketing by showcasing the faces behind your clinic. People connect with people, so make sure your team is visible on your website and social media. This builds trust and makes your clinic more approachable.

Invest in paid advertising. Paid advertising, like Google Ads, is crucial for maintaining consistent client flow. Spend wisely, track your results, and don't hesitate to invest in strategies that bring measurable returns.

Diversify your marketing channels. Don't rely on a single marketing channel. Use a combination of tactics – Google Ads, social media, local events, and more – to ensure you're visible to potential clients in multiple ways.

Consistency is key. Marketing isn't a one-off task. Consistent, repeated exposure across various platforms is necessary to make a lasting impression on potential clients. Aim for visibility in at least seven different ways.

Track and measure your efforts. Always track the results of your marketing efforts. Knowing what works allows you to focus your resources on strategies that deliver the best returns, ensuring your marketing is both effective and efficient. Marketing is the lifeblood of your clinic. It's not just about being seen, it's about being seen by the right people, in the right way, at the right time.

By understanding your ideal client, crafting a message that resonates, and being consistently visible across multiple channels, you'll position your clinic for sustained success. Remember, visibility is currency – protect and nurture it with a strategic, multi-channel approach. Your marketing should be a conversation with your ideal clients, addressing their needs and showing them that you are the expert they've been looking for. With these strategies in place, your clinic will not only attract more clients but will also stand out in a crowded market, ensuring steady growth and a thriving business.

8

The Growth Rings of Success

Running a successful clinic requires more than just clinical expertise. Yes, that is an essential part of course, but we have to understand the "business side of things," which, unfortunately, many clinic owners overlook. With many graduating therapists now setting up their own practice, surely this is something that ought to be added to the curriculum. Anyway, I won't get on my soapbox about that!

In the hustle and bustle of daily operations, it's easy to focus solely on client care and leave the numbers to chance. But what we see happening is this: You submit your pile of receipts to the accountant at the end of the year and a few months later, they send you your P&L and self-assessment, and this is when you see how well – or "not well" – you did last year.

This is often when you start thinking you might be better off getting a "normal" job, or when you realise you are the worst-paid person in your clinic. This accounting method, or really, the way of using your bank account to assess the health of your clinic, is a recipe for disaster.

Understanding your metrics is crucial. Running a clinic can provide you with a handsome income, it can give you time and flexibility in your life and it can provide huge fulfilment. But for us to achieve this, we need to dive into our numbers. So, let's do this now!

Let me take you back a few years to when I first opened my own clinic. Like many of you, I was excited, passionate and ready to make a difference in the lives of my clients. I was confident in my ability to provide top-notch care. But when it came to the business side, I was a little less sure-footed. I thought if I just focused on my clients, everything else would fall into place.

For the first few months, things seemed to be going well. The clinic was really busy, clients were happy and I felt like I was making an impact. But then the bills started piling up and I realised Bupa and AXA would take an age to pay. I remember thinking, "Hmmm, potential cash flow issue right there!" I quickly needed to hire staff, but I had no idea what my margins were, so how could I make the right decision on what to pay them? This is where the 50/50 split is crazy for freelance staff. Most clinic owners use this pay system only because it's how it has always been, *not* because it's what the business can afford. This is especially frustrating as our cost of delivery has jumped up so much in the last five years. At that point, I also had instructors teaching classes – but I had no idea how many bums on mats I needed for this service to make money. Then there was the small issue of needing to eat and pay my bills!

The turning point came when I got to chatting with a client whose knee I was treating. Terry – who has let me use his real name here – was asking me lots of questions about my new business, and he was explaining what his job had been before he retired. He was a numbers genius, and in addition to that, a whizz at Excel! He kindly agreed to sit down with me and create my business a scorecard, which would have everything I really needed to look at and know. And this was the moment I started to love numbers. I had told myself for years I was rubbish at maths, needing a tutor at GCSE, and generally hating every minute of learning the Pythagorean theorem (which I've still never used in my adult life!).

I became numbers-obsessed. Every decision I made in the business was based on what the numbers were telling me. I looked at the numbers to help me decide everything: when to hire, when to fire, when to raise prices, how much to pay someone, how many clients I needed, how much to spend on equipment, how much to set aside for taxes, how much each patient was worth to the business – and most importantly, how much money we could make before I needed to think about getting a bigger clinic! This number was staggering: £1 million! Yes, that's right, my upside potential was a £1 million Great British Pounds.

We hit six figures *and* made profit in year one, plus every year since, and I've been able to pay myself regularly since then, too. This was true even in 2020, when 65% of our services had to shut down for various periods of time. Because I had absolute clarity on my numbers, I knew what I needed to do.

It's easy to fall into the trap of thinking that numbers are just for accountants. But the truth is, if you're not paying attention to your clinic's metrics, you're putting your business at risk. Numbers don't lie – they tell the story of your clinic's health, and it's up to you to listen.

Ignoring your numbers is like driving a car with your eyes closed. You might get by for a while, but sooner or later, you're going to crash. Many clinic owners I've worked with have made the same mistake I did, burying their heads in the sand when it comes to metrics. They focus on client care, which is undeniably important, but they forget that without a healthy business, they wouldn't be able to care for anyone.

Every clinic owner should have some form of accounting software; whether it's Xero or QuickBooks, you should be using it. This makes your life a lot easier, and your accountant's! It gives you daily oversight on your numbers, and that is whether you are a sole trader or a big clinic owner.

Secondly, get a great accountant, ideally one that runs the Profit First model. If you are reading this book and doing your own accounts, please stop! We would not try to MOT our own car, or fit our own underfloor heating, or service our own boiler, so why do we think – and usually just to save some money! – that we can do our own accounts?

However, if you are a trained accountant in a past life, then knock yourself out doing the numbers.

"What metrics or numbers do I need to know, Katie?" you ask. Well, the bigger the business, the more things you will need to and want to know, but let me give you the minimum.

Key Metrics You Need to Know and Track

Revenue and Profit Margins. Revenue is the lifeblood of your clinic, but profit margins are where true financial health lies. Understanding your margins helps you determine if your pricing and cost management strategies are effective.

Cash Flow. Cash flow is critical to keeping your clinic running smoothly. Positive cash flow ensures you can cover expenses, pay your staff, and invest in growth opportunities. This is so important when you work with insurance companies or case managers.

Patient Retention Rate. Retaining patients is more cost-effective than constantly acquiring new ones. A high retention rate indicates patient satisfaction and loyalty, which are crucial for long-term success.

New Patient Acquisition Rate. While retention is important, so is attracting new patients. This metric helps you understand how effective your marketing and outreach efforts are in bringing new clients to your clinic.

Appointment Booking Rate. Your appointment booking rate reflects the efficiency of your scheduling process. High booking rates mean that your clinic is operating at or near capacity, maximising revenue potential.

Average Revenue Per Patient. This metric helps you understand the financial contribution of each patient. It can and should guide decisions on your acquisition cost.

Expense Ratios. Tracking your expenses in relation to your revenue helps you identify areas where you can cut costs without compromising the quality of care.

Conversion Rate. Measuring new patients to follow-up conversion rate will help you identify which staff members you need to support and coach to build their confidence, and if this is a problem, your marketing spend is wasted! This is also relevant if you have an administrative team.

Let me share the story of another client of ours who we'll call Sarah. Sarah is an excellent sports therapist who was facing similar challenges. Her clinic was becoming busier, and she was known for her exceptional patient care.

However, she had drawn out more money than she should have because she didn't know her numbers, and she had staff taking home a full-time equivalent rate of £97,500 per year. You might find yourself doing this too if you pay high hourly rates!

When we first met, Sarah was at her wit's end. She was working long hours, but her clinic's financial performance didn't reflect her efforts.

I asked her a simple question: "Do you know your numbers?" Sarah admitted that she didn't. She had been so focused on treating patients that she hadn't paid attention to the financial aspects of her business.

Together, we began to dig into her clinic's metrics. We looked at everything: revenue, expenses, patient retention, appointment booking rates, and more. It was a daunting process at first, but Sarah quickly saw the value in it. We identified areas where she was losing money, such as unbilled appointments and underpriced services. By making a few strategic changes, Sarah was able to turn things around.

Within a few months, Sarah's clinic was not only stable but profitable. She had a clear understanding of her financial position and the confidence to make decisions that supported her long-term goals. Today, Sarah's clinic continues to thrive, and she credits her success to understanding and acting on her metrics.

This is why your master plan is crucial, it allows you to set the growth plan for your business, and then assess all the metrics surrounding that to decide what actions you need to take first. My rule is, if it's not moving you towards the goal, you don't do it!

In the journey to growing your clinic, understanding your metrics is not an option – it's a necessity. Your numbers are more than just figures, they are the pulse of your business. By embracing this aspect of your clinic, you gain control, clarity, and confidence.

You can make informed decisions that lead to sustainable growth and long-term success. Remember, the branches of your clinic's success tree are only as strong as the foundation they're built on. By grounding your practice in solid metrics, you ensure that your clinic not only survives but thrives.

9

The Leadership Canopy

Our next branch is team management. I have to say, this is my favourite, so buckle up as it's juicy! This branch supports everything else.

A clinic is only as strong as the people who work within it, and without a cohesive, skilled, and motivated team, even the best-laid plans can fall apart.

I want you to start and finish this chapter thinking *who*, not *how*! Let me explain....

If you are a sole trader and think this chapter is not for you, I would encourage you to go ahead and read it. The principles we are going to look at will help you lead in all aspects of your life, and show you how you can shift your mindset from being the one that has to do it all – yes, even in your home and personal life! – to get people around you to support you, so you can live the life you love and not settle for anything less. Because this is why we run a business.

For many clinic owners, team management is both the most rewarding and the most challenging aspect of running a business. You're not just managing a group of employees, you're cultivating a team that shares your vision, works together towards common goals and ultimately helps your clinic thrive. This branch of the tree is about more than just hiring the right people – it's about leading them effectively, creating an environment where they can excel and eventually stepping back so that the clinic can operate smoothly without your constant oversight, so you can take mini-retirements!

In this chapter, we'll dive into the key components of building and managing a world-class team for your clinic and your life. I'll share my personal journey in hiring, leading and eventually stepping back from day-to-day operations – a journey that transformed my clinic and my life. You'll learn the strategies I used to attract top talent, the leadership principles that helped me foster a high-performance culture and the systems I put in place to ensure the clinic could run like a well-oiled machine, even in my absence.

Building a World-Class Team

When I first started my clinic, like many clinic owners, I wore all the hats. I was the therapist, the manager, the marketer, the receptionist and everything in between. At first, it seemed like the only way to get things done. After all, who else could understand my vision or execute it as well as I could? But as the clinic grew, it became clear that this approach wasn't sustainable. I was burnt out, and the clinic's growth was starting to plateau because I simply didn't have the capacity to do it all. That's when I realised that to take my clinic to the next level, I needed to build a team that could share the load – and not just any team, but a world-class one.

I remember the exact moment when I knew something had to change. It was a Friday evening, and I was the last one in the clinic …again! I was exhausted, staring at a mountain of admin work that had piled up throughout the week. Patients were happy, but I was drowning in tasks that were pulling me away from what I loved most – treating clients and growing the business. My personal life was suffering, and I knew deep down that if I didn't find a way to delegate and trust others to handle parts of the business, I was going to burn out completely. I had this big realisation that I needed to get a team if I really wanted to help more people.

Step One: Hiring with Intention

Hiring the right people is one of the most critical steps in building a successful team. It isn't just about finding therapists with the right qualifications or administrators who have the right skills. It is about finding those who are a perfect fit for the culture in your company, those who align with your values – remember those, we got clear on them in the trunk section! – and those who are wired for the role.

We have a 12-step hiring process that we encourage our clients in Thrive to follow. It's a game changer for hiring and onboarding your team in the way that sets them up for success. Here, I share with you two vital steps from our 12-step process, which will transform the way you hire people.

First, remember that your time is precious. It's worth a lot of money, so use it wisely. Run 10-minute introductory interviews with the people you have shortlisted from the applications. This saves you time and effort, and in my opinion, for you to warrant giving up a lot of time to run the face-to-face interview, they need to be blooming good! This gives you a great opportunity to quickly assess if they share the values you are looking for, whether they have done their research on your company, and for you to decide whether they are right to progress to the next stage. And by the way, that next stage is still not meeting you face to face!

Second, remember that strength testing is worth its weight in gold. There are many different assessments out there, but this really helps recruit someone who is wired for the specific role you are looking for. This is about getting the right person in the right seat. This, in my opinion, is where so many companies go wrong. They promote internally due to length of service, rather than where their employees' strengths lie and what the role requires. This is something we get all of our clients to do when they join our program too. It allows us to support them in hiring the people they need, coach them and support them based on how they are wired. This is why we get such incredible results with our clients. Everyone is unique, and every business is unique.

Hiring is about being clear on your values and company culture. Even if you are working on your own in your business, you can effectively delegate tasks to a VA or employ a cleaner to help you out. My cleaners at home and business align with my values, hence they are a great fit and I never have any issues and they meet my expectations every time.

Step Two: Becoming a World-Class Leader

Effective leadership and management are the twin pillars of a successful organisation. But before we dive into the specifics, it's important to understand the distinction between leadership and management.

Leadership is about providing direction, inspiring the team and setting a vision that aligns with the company's core values and long-term goals. It involves the ability to motivate and influence others to achieve their highest potential. This is the visionary's role – which is often you, as the clinic owner!

Management focuses on the execution of the vision through planning, organising and overseeing the day-to-day operations. Managers ensure that the team is following processes, hitting targets and maintaining consistency. This would be the role of the business manager or operations manager. Now you might be sitting in both of those seats right now, so don't panic, this is about looking at what you may need as your clinic grows. It's crucial that you switch hats effectively depending on the situation.

There are many tools and tactics to becoming an inspiring leader, and I could write a book on that in itself. That could be my next one! But the key thing to think about in your organisation, whether you have 2, 10, or 50 people in it, is first you need an Accountability Chart.

This tool helps in clearly defining roles and responsibilities within the team. Unlike a traditional organisational chart, the Accountability Chart focuses on who is accountable for what. Leaders and managers use this to ensure everyone knows their role and what they are responsible for, reducing overlap and confusion. If you work with your partner in the business – I use this example as we have so many couples in Thrive – this becomes even more important.

In addition to this, Key Performance Indicators (KPIs) are crucial for both performance management and making informed decisions about firing because they provide objective, measurable data on an employee's effectiveness in their role. These also form the basis of your appraisals.

Leaders need to learn to speak less and listen more, empower their team to succeed and always refer back to the company's vision and core values.

Delegate, Delete, or Do

Leadership is about more than just giving orders; it's about inspiring your team to take ownership of the roles and responsibilities that you have set out.

Give your team the autonomy to make decisions within their areas of responsibility as defined in the Accountability Chart. This empowerment fosters a sense of ownership and motivation.

I found this hard, because not only am I a recovering people pleaser, I am also a recovering perfectionist. This means delegating and passing over control of tasks can be hard. Does this sound familiar to you too?

A critical mindset shift for leaders is realising that they don't need to know everything. Instead, they should surround themselves with people who have the expertise they lack.

Renowned entrepreneur Richard Branson embodies this approach. Early in his career, Branson admitted that he didn't understand what "P&L" (Profit and Loss) meant. Rather than seeing this as a limitation, he focused on building a team of knowledgeable individuals who could fill in his gaps. By empowering experts and relying on their strengths, Branson was able to focus on his own talents, like visionary thinking and risk-taking, which helped him grow the Virgin empire. His story illustrates that leadership is not about having all the answers, but about building a team that collectively does. However, I will caveat this story, as there are certain things you definitely need to know as a leader (and that's your numbers!).

Your Time is Worth Money

Perhaps you feel like you are constantly spinning a lot of plates, never have enough time, and are not often present at home. Running a time analysis, every quarter is essential to get yourself out of the day-to-day operations and make sure your time is being spent in the areas that are going to make the biggest difference to the business.

Put very simply, you can work out how much your time is worth in the business, clinically and non-clinically. For example, let's assume you can make £100 an hour when you are seeing clients. That then means any task you are doing that could be done by someone else for less than £100 needs to be delegated! The other powerful thing that comes out of this activity is seeing what you need to delete. What are you doing that is not making you money or getting you closer to your goal?

One of the reasons I think this area is often the biggest challenge for clinic owners is that leaders have to be committed to their growth, as well as that of their team. We spend so long working on our clinical skills and doing endless courses (which I am not against), that we tend to forget to upskill ourselves in the areas of business management and leadership. A part of that entails looking at our time in a ruthless way so you can create a profitable business.

Step Three: Creating Systems for Success

Building a world-class team is one thing, but ensuring they can work effectively without your constant oversight is another challenge entirely. For my clinic to truly thrive, I needed to step back from the day-to-day operations and trust my team to manage things on their own. This required creating systems that empowered my team to make decisions, solve problems and keep the clinic running smoothly.

I started by documenting all the critical processes in the clinic. This included everything from patient intake procedures to how we handled billing and insurance claims. By having these processes clearly outlined, I was able to ensure consistency in how things were done, even when I wasn't directly involved.

Next, I focused on training and development. I wanted to equip my team with the skills and knowledge they needed to excel in their roles. This meant investing in ongoing education and professional development opportunities, as well as providing regular feedback and coaching. I also encouraged a culture of continuous improvement, where team members were always looking for ways to enhance their skills and contribute to the clinic's success.

The accountability chart with defined roles and responsibilities helped eliminate confusion and ensured that everyone knew who was responsible for what. It also allowed me to delegate more effectively as

I could assign tasks and projects to the team members best suited for them.

Finally, I implemented a regular meeting rhythm to keep everyone on the same page and foster open communication. These meetings were an opportunity to review progress, discuss any issues that had come up, and brainstorm solutions as a group. They also helped reinforce the sense of teamwork and shared purpose that I wanted to cultivate in the clinic.

Step Four: Letting Go and Stepping Back

Perhaps the hardest part of this journey was learning to let go. As a clinic owner, it's easy to fall into the trap of thinking that you need to be involved in every decision and every detail. But to truly build a successful clinic, you need to trust your team and give them the space to take ownership of their work.

For me, this meant gradually stepping back from the day-to-day operations and focusing more on strategic planning and growth. I started by delegating smaller tasks and gradually increased the level of responsibility I gave to my team. Over time, I was able to remove myself from the day-to-day entirely, knowing that my team had the skills, systems, and support they needed to keep the clinic running smoothly.

This was a game-changer, not just for the clinic but for my personal life as well. By freeing up my time, I was able to focus on new opportunities for growth, both professionally and personally. I could invest in expanding the clinic, explore new business ventures (hence I am writing this book), and spend more time with my friends and family.

I took my first mini-retirement in the third year of owning my clinic, where I went around the world and took a full month away. This is a great way to stress test your business. Your business needs to run without you, otherwise you have a job.

The Results: A Thriving Clinic and a Balanced Life

We've been working with another of our Elevate clients, who we'll call Steph, to lessen her clinical workload and help remove herself from the day-to-day operations. Since we started the process in the last 12 months, she has taken more unplugged holidays than ever before, she's been able to go to school sports days and is more present in the evening with family. But that's only half of it. Her income has grown and her clients are happier than ever.

To do this, Steph had to get really clear on the roles and responsibilities of each of her team members. She had to communicate the vision well and consistently. She had to delegate and empower her team to make decisions without her. Steph has been able to grow her clinics in ways that she would never have been able to do holding on to every element!

In the next chapter, we'll explore the final branch of the Clinic Success Tree: Operations. We'll look at how to create a systems-driven business so that you can step back and enjoy the fruits of this tree we have been creating since the beginning of this book.

10
Cultivating the Systems Branch

Let's face it, you likely started this business by taking a risk, doing things when they needed to get done, and not necessarily doing anything in order or from a standard operating procedure (SOP).

But this is often where we encounter a crucial turning point – a moment when the chaos of day-to-day operations begins to overshadow the purpose and vision that originally drove you to start your clinic.

As clinic owners, we start with enthusiasm, a desire to make a difference and the ambition to build a successful business. However, without the right systems in place, the clinic can quickly become a source of stress rather than fulfilment. This is so often the place everyone is in when they reach out for help with us. They have lost sight of the why and are buried in day-to-day operations and on the brink of burnout.

For you to make more money, get your life back, and have things run smoothly, this now must change. You cannot be in the weeds and planting the garden at the same time.

This chapter is dedicated to the final branch of the Clinic Success Tree: Systems. Just as a tree relies on its branches to spread out and thrive, a clinic depends on robust systems and processes to function efficiently and grow sustainably.

Systems are the lifeblood of your clinic. So, buckle up, we are about to turn your business into a finely tuned machine.

The Turning Point with Systems

Do you find yourself at these crossroads every few years?

A period of growth has happened, and you look around and the to-do list has grown... again! It feels like as you grow, the list never gets any smaller. It just seems to get bigger and the chance of having protected time or an unplugged holiday is slim. Or if you do manage to do that, you come back to a gigantic pile of work, making you wonder if having a holiday is even worthwhile.

Let me ask you this: What would happen if you took a week away from your business, completely unplugged? What about a month? What about three months?

Several years ago, I decided to take a mini-retirement for a month, and this meant everything on my to-do list needed to go! It forced me to put a process in place for everything I touched. Now as a visionary, this is utterly boring for me to do, but I needed to do it so the business would continue to not only run but thrive without me. So, as I set about putting systems and processes in place, my rule was this: Anything that happened more than once needed an SOP. By the way, we made more net profit that month I was out than any other month up to that point.

That was the moment I realised I needed to not return to micro-managing every single thing!

The Power of Systems in Action

Let me share with you a story about John, who also faced a similar challenge in his physiotherapy clinic. John was an exceptional physiotherapist with a passion for helping his patients, but he struggled with the operational side of his business. His clinic was always busy, but he felt like he was constantly putting out fires: dealing with staff issues, attempting marketing, and trying to keep up with the endless stream of administrative tasks.

When John came to me, he was on the brink of burnout. He loved his work but hated the chaos that seemed to come with running the clinic. We began by assessing his current systems – or lack thereof – and identifying the areas that needed the most attention. One of the first things we tackled was his patient enquiry and booking process, which was disorganised and time-consuming. By implementing a simple, streamlined system for this, we were able to reduce errors, speed up the process, and improve the patient experience.

Next, we focused on his staff management. John had a great team, but without clear systems in place, they often felt overwhelmed and uncertain about their roles. We introduced regular team meetings, established clear protocols for communication and created detailed job descriptions for each role. These changes not only improved efficiency but also boosted team morale and reduced turnover.

Over time, John's clinic transformed. What was once a chaotic and stressful environment became a well-oiled machine. His clinic grew, his patients were happier and most importantly, John rediscovered his passion for his work. He was no longer bogged down by the day-to-day operations and could focus on what truly mattered – providing excellent care to his patients.

John's success story is a testament to the power of systems in a clinic. When you take the time to create and implement effective systems, the results are profound. Not only does your clinic run more smoothly, but you also gain the freedom to focus on growth and innovation.

John is also now playing much more golf!

No matter how small or big your clinic, the mindset you must embrace is, "I am the leader of a process-driven company." If we had all done this earlier in our business, we would have created a much more streamlined, effective, profitable, and fulfilling business.

Systems enhance consistency and quality control. They ensure that tasks are performed consistently and to a high standard every time so you don't have to keep checking if someone is doing it. How would that feel? Good, right?

The Benefits of Effective Systems

Systems improve efficiency and time management. With effective systems, tasks that once took hours can be completed in minutes. This not only improves your clinic's efficiency but also frees up your time to focus on strategic activities (or more golf!).

They allow your clinic to scale. As your clinic grows, the demands on your time and resources will increase. Systems allow you to scale your operations without losing control. They provide a framework that supports growth and ensures that your clinic can handle increased patient volumes and staff numbers without compromising on quality.

They empower your team. When your team knows exactly what is expected of them and they have clear guidelines to follow, they are more confident and empowered in their roles. This leads to higher job satisfaction, better performance, and reduced staff turnover.

Now admittedly this can feel like a huge task, and is why creating an operations manual is seen as not urgent and pushed to the back burner, collecting dust. We spend a full day with our members during our strategy days on this very thing, the operations manual!

This allows our Elevate members to leverage their time, energy, money, and staff, creating game-changing results in their business and life. Let me share a couple of simple steps you can take to start creating a system-driven clinic.

First, understand that you are not the one to create or run the Operations Manual. Hurrah! Yes, everything needs to be documented, but you don't have to be the one to do it. You just need to create the shell of it. Your job is to help define the processes that must be outlined, as well as a deadline by which they must be documented. Then it's every team member's job to document each procedure as they do it each time.

If it is only you in your business, you will of course create fewer systems. I urge you to use technology to optimise how you do things so you can have more time back to either see more clients or enjoy your life!

For those who are thinking, "But, Katie, I am doing loads of processes and tasks in the business, so it will have to be me who does that," here is a simple way.

This is *not* about creating another job on your to-do list. After all, you're already doing the things you need to document. This is *not* about creating processes for things that don't currently happen in your business.

So, a simple step is that the next time you do the task, record your screen and talk over it, or grab your phone and record a walkthrough. For example, next time you open up the clinic in the morning, just record yourself doing it! If you do this consistently over a few months, you will have created many systems and processes that you can keep in a Google Drive folder you can name "Operations Manual."

My second tip would be to understand that with the right systems, you can be high-touch in a high-tech world.

Sometimes, we are afraid to create systems in our business because we pride ourselves on special touches or personal care. Making clients feel important is a really crucial part of running a successful clinic and has a very positive long-term impact. The problem is that many of you are initiating them personally. This is okay in the beginning, but not when you are seeing more than 50 clients a week, or when you take on new members and you want to ensure quality across the team.

The feel-good actions should absolutely continue, but they too can be put into a predictable, well-thought-out process, such as automated birthday messages or member packs for new clients.

By the way, when you get into this habit, your personal life operates in a much more streamlined fashion too.

Take out your journal, and list the top five things that take up time, happen often and have a big impact on the running of the clinic. These are the tasks that, with a process, you could confidently delegate and trust they can be done.

The Foundation for Long-Term Success

Remember, the Systems Branch of your Clinic Success Tree is what ties everything together. It supports the other branches – sales, marketing, team and numbers – and ensures that they can all function harmoniously. Without strong systems, even the best strategies can falter.

As you move forward, keep in mind that building systems is an ongoing process. It requires continuous evaluation, refinement, and adaptation to meet the changing needs of your clinic. But the rewards are well worth it. With a solid foundation of systems in place, you can take your clinic to new heights, achieve your business goals, and most importantly, create a clinic environment where both you and your clients thrive.

Your journey towards a process-driven clinic starts today. Take that first step, and watch your clinic transform into a thriving, efficient, and successful business that stands the test of time.

Conclusion
Harvesting the Fruits of Your Clinic Success Tree

As we reach the final chapter of our journey together, it's time to look up and see the fruits of your labour or the pretty pink blossom – the rewards that come from nurturing your Clinic Success Tree from the roots to the branches. The blossoms are what makes all the effort worthwhile, and they represent the true essence of success: time, energy, money and confidence.

Success in running a clinic – or any business, for that matter – is deeply personal. It's not a one-size-fits-all destination. Just as no two trees produce the same fruit, the rewards of your work will be unique to you. This chapter is about recognising and embracing the fruits of your success while encouraging you to dream bigger, to want more from your life and to understand that running a clinic doesn't mean settling for an average life.

From Roots to Fruits

The Clinic Success Tree is a holistic model that starts from the roots - your personal performance and mindset - and grows through the trunk of values, master plan, and strategy. The branches – team, marketing, sales, operations, and numbers – represent the different aspects of your clinic that you've nurtured along the way. Each part of the tree is crucial, and together, they form the foundation for the fruits you now see.

The Roots: Personal Performance and Mindset

Your journey began with you - your mindset, your values, and your personal performance. These roots are the foundation of everything else. They anchor you, give you stability, and allow you to weather the storms of business and life. Without strong roots, even the most impressive tree will struggle to survive, let alone bear fruit.

The Trunk: Values, Master Plan and Strategy

The trunk of your Clinic Success Tree represents your clinic's core – your values, master plan, and strategy.

This is where you define what your clinic stands for, where it's headed, and how it will get there. A strong trunk supports the entire structure, ensuring that your clinic grows in the right direction and remains true to its purpose.

The Branches: Team, Marketing, Sales, Operations and Numbers

The branches are the operational aspects of your clinic – the team that supports you, the marketing that brings in clients, the sales strategies that drive revenue, the systems and operations that keep everything running smoothly, and the numbers that track your progress. Each branch plays a vital role in the overall health and growth of your clinic.

When you take the time to nurture each of these elements, you create a clinic that not only survives but thrives. And when your clinic thrives, you begin to experience the fruits of your labour.

The Fruits of Success: Time, Energy, Money and Confidence

Success, as I've mentioned, is deeply personal. For some, it's about financial freedom, for others, it's about having more time with family, feeling energised by their work or gaining the confidence to take on new challenges. The fruits of your Clinic Success Tree represent these rewards – time, energy, money and confidence.

Time. Time is one of the most valuable resources we have, yet it's often the first thing we sacrifice in the pursuit of success. When your clinic is running smoothly, supported by strong roots and a well-structured trunk, you gain more control over your time. You're no longer chained to the daily grind, constantly putting out fires and dealing with crises. Instead, you have the freedom to spend your time where it matters most, whether that's with your family, pursuing hobbies or simply taking a well-deserved break.

Energy. Running a clinic can be exhausting, both physically and mentally. But when you have a solid team, efficient systems, and a clear strategy, you're able to conserve your energy. You're not constantly drained by the day-to-day operations, instead, you're energised by the knowledge that your clinic is thriving. You can put your energy into the areas where you have the most impact, whether that's patient care, business development or personal growth.

Money. Let's talk about money. While it's not the only measure of success, it's certainly an important one. Financial stability allows you to invest in your clinic, your team and your own life. It gives you the freedom to make choices, to take risks.

However, it's important to recognise that not everyone achieves significant financial success. Statistics show that only about 9% of small business owners earn six figures or more annually. This is the minority, but the choice is yours. You've already taken steps to build a strong foundation with your Clinic Success Tree, and with the right mindset and strategies, you can join that 9%. Remember though that money is just one aspect of success. It's the means, not the end.

Confidence. Finally, there's confidence – the belief in yourself and your ability to succeed. Confidence comes from knowing that you've built something strong, something that can weather challenges and continue to grow.

When you have a clinic that runs like a well-oiled machine, backed by solid systems and a clear strategy, you naturally feel more confident. This confidence spills over into every area of your life, empowering you to take on new challenges, make bold decisions, and dream bigger.

Dream Bigger: The Thrive Stretcher

As you stand at the edge of your clinic's success, I want to encourage you to stretch, to dream bigger, and to want more from your life. It's easy to fall into the trap of thinking that running a clinic means accepting a life of stress, long hours and just getting by. But that doesn't have to be your reality.

The Thrive Stretcher is a mindset tool I want you to adopt. It's about pushing the boundaries of what you believe is possible, both for your clinic and for your life. Ask yourself: What does your ideal life look like? How can your clinic be a vehicle to help you achieve that life? What would it take to make that vision a reality?

Success is not just about surviving – it's about thriving. It's about creating a life that excites you, that gives you the freedom to pursue your passions and that allows you to make a meaningful impact on the world. Whether it's financial abundance, time freedom, personal fulfilment or all of the above, the choice is yours.

Success Is Unique to You

It's important to remember that success is not a one-size-fits-all concept. The fruits of your Clinic Success Tree will be different from those of your peers, and that's perfectly okay. For some, success might mean building a clinic empire with multiple locations and a seven-figure income. For others, it might mean running a single clinic that provides a comfortable living while allowing for a balanced lifestyle.

Money isn't everything, and it's certainly not the only measure of success. True success is about living a life that aligns with your values, that brings you joy and fulfilment, and that allows you to make a positive impact on the people around you.

As you reflect on the fruits of your success, take the time to define what success means to you. What are the most important rewards for you? Is it financial security? More time with loved ones? The energy to pursue your passions? The confidence to take on new challenges?

Whatever your definition of success, remember that it's yours to create. You have the power to shape your life and your clinic in a way that aligns with your vision and values.

The Journey Continues

As we conclude this book, I want to leave you with this thought: The journey doesn't end here. The Clinic Success Tree is not a static model – it's a living, growing entity that requires ongoing care and attention. As your clinic evolves, so too will your goals, challenges and definitions of success. Keep nurturing your roots – your personal performance and mindset. Continue to strengthen your trunk – your values, master plan, and strategy. And always pay attention to your branches – your team, marketing, sales, operations, and numbers. By doing so, you'll ensure that your Clinic Success Tree continues to bear fruit, year after year.

Thank you for allowing me to be a part of your journey. I'm excited about what the future holds for you and your clinic. Dream big, stretch yourself, and never settle for an average life. The fruits of your success are within reach – go out and harvest them.

What's Next for You

From these pages, you have gained some insight into the specific mindset needed to make the changes we have discussed. We have delved into the tactics and the how-to, but actually making this happen is a whole different ball game.

Helping people like you is what we do day in and out and in the Thrive coaching programs. This is where successful clinic owners are made – and beautiful trees, too! – with support, accountability, and a community to champion you.

Is this program right for you? If you have made it to this point in the book, you have the staying power, commitment, and attitude to become hugely successful. We all know that it's hard to see the blind spots in your own business, and we can lose steam, talk ourselves out of things, get busy being busy and stay where we are.

If you're like me and the thought of moving forward on your own feels too big and overwhelming, I have two suggestions below.

Take the Clinic Health Check

The free clinic health check will show you exactly how your clinic is performing in all the key areas we discussed in this book, and give you an idea of what to focus on first. The assessment takes three minutes on average and we will send you your results once done.

To take the Clinic Health check, go to: https://bizhealthcheck.scoreapp.com or simply scan the QR code below.

Book a Free Discovery Session

Let's book you a free call with one of my amazing coaches. They have all run businesses in the health and wellness industry, understand exactly where you might be experiencing challenges, and can help you map out a plan of action whilst exploring with you what it would look like for us to work together.

Time and time again, I have found that just one conversation can change your life for the better. This may be it. Everything you discuss is kept completely confidential. We are here with a compassionate ear to listen to your particular struggles with zero judgement. We have all been there! Believe me!

Scan the QR code below or head to this link https://call.thrive-businesscoaching.com/discovery-call and answer a few simple questions. This will get us on our way to solving your biggest challenges and get you on the right track with support, accountability and community.

Recommended Readings

Atomic Habits: An Easy & Proven Way to Build Good Habits & Break Bad Ones by James Clear

Breaking the Habit of Being Yourself by Dr. Joe Dispenza

Excuse Me, Your Life Is Waiting, Expanded Study Edition: The Astonishing Power of Feelings by Lynn Grabhorn

Psycho-Cybernetics by Maxwell Maltz

Secrets of the Millionaire Mind: Mastering the Inner Game of Wealth by T. Harv Eker

The Body Keeps the Score: Brain, Mind, and Body in the Healing of Trauma by Bessel Van Der Kolk, M.D.

The Slight Edge: Turning Simple Disciplines into Massive Success and Happiness by Jeff Olson

You Are a Badass® at Making Money: Master the Mindset of Wealth by Jen Sincero

You Are a Badass®: How to Stop Doubting Your Greatness and Start Living an Awesome Life by Jen Sincero

References

[1] R.M. Brown, *Sudden Death,* U.S., Bantam, 1983.

[2] M. Michaelowicz, *Profit First: Transform Your Business from a Cash-Eating Monster to a Money-Making Machine (Entrepreneurship Simplified).* U.S., Portfolio., 2017.

Printed in Great Britain
by Amazon